The Age
of

PARADOX

The Age
of
PARADOX

CHARLES HANDY

Harvard Business School Press
Boston, Massachusetts

First published in the United States by the Harvard Business School Press in hard cover, 1994; in paperback, 1995

First published in Great Britain by The Random House UK Limited, 1994, as *The Empty Raincoat*

Printed in the United States of America

99 98 97 96 95   5 4 3 2 1 (pbk)

Library of Congress Cataloging-in-Publication Data

Handy, Charles B.
    The age of paradox / Charles Handy.
        p. cm.
    Includes bibliographical references and index.
    ISBN 0–87584–425–1 (hc)
    ISBN 0–87584–643–2 (pbk)
    1. Organizational change.   2. Organizational behavior.   3. Social
prediction.   I. Title.
    HD58.8.H3618 1994
    302.3′5—dc20   93–36586
                                                                              CIP

The paper used in this publication meets the requirements of the American National Standard for Permanence of Paper for Printed Library Materials Z39.49–1984.

Contents

Contents

Preface

Four years ago, my earlier book, *The Age of Unreason,* was published. In that book I presented a view of the way work was being re-shaped and the effect that the re-shaping might have on our lives. It was, on the whole, an optimistic view and an upbeat book. Since then, the world of work has changed very much along the lines described in the book. This should be comforting to an author, but I have not found it so. Too many people and institutions have been unsettled by the changes. Capitalism has not proved as flexible as it was supposed to be, governments have not been all wise or far seeing. Life is a struggle for many and a puzzle for most.

It has not turned out to be as simple or as easy as I had thought. What is happening in our mature societies is much more fundamental, confusing, and distressing than I had expected. It is that confusion which I am addressing in this book. Part of the confusion stems from our pursuit of efficiency and economic growth, in the conviction that these are the necessary ingredients of progress. In the pursuit of these goals we can be tempted to forget that it is we, individual men and women, who should be the measure of all things, not made to measure for something else. It is easy to lose ourselves in efficiency, to treat that efficiency as an end in itself and not a means to other ends.

I cannot forget a sculpture I saw in the open-air sculpture garden in Minneapolis—"Without Words" by Judith Shea. There are three shapes. One of them, the dominant one, is a bronze raincoat, standing upright, hands in pockets, but empty, with no one inside. To me, that empty raincoat is the symbol of our most pressing paradox. We were not destined to be empty raincoats, nameless numbers on a payroll, role occupants, the raw material of economics or sociology, statistics in a government report. If that is to be its price, economic progress is an empty promise. There must be more to life than being a cog in someone else's great machine, hurtling God knows where. The challenge must be to prove that the paradox can be managed and that each one of us can fill that empty raincoat.

I have called my new book *The Age of Paradox* because so many things, just now, seem to contain their own contradictions, so many good intentions to have unintended consequences, and so many formulas for success to carry a sting in their tail. Paradox has almost become the cliché of our times. The word crops up again and again as people look for a way to describe the dilemmas facing governments, businesses, and, increasingly, individuals. Sometimes it seems that the more we know, the more confused we get; that the more we increase our technical capacity, the more powerless we become. With all our sophisticated armaments we can only watch impotently while parts of the world kill each other. We grow more food than we need but cannot feed the starving. We can unravel the mysteries of the galaxies but not of our own families. To call it paradox, however, is only to label it, not to deal with it. We have to find ways to make sense of the paradoxes, to use them to shape a better destiny.

I know precisely when paradox became the key concept in my search for a way out of the confusions. It was in Sausalito, California, when John O'Neil gave me the first chapter of his new book to read. John is president of the California School of Professional Psychology, a wise and shrewd observer, and counsellor to leaders and organizations. The book was called *The Paradox of Success* and subtitled *When Winning at Work Means Losing at Life*. The book is about the personal dilemmas of leadership, but the important message for me was that there are never any simple or right answers in any part of life. I used to think that there were, or could be. I now see paradoxes everywhere I look. Every coin, I now realize, has at least two sides, but there are pathways through the paradoxes if we can understand what is happening and are prepared to act differently.

The ideas in my last book are still relevant; organizations will become both smaller and bigger at the same time; they will be flatter, more flexible, and more dispersed; similarly our working lives will have to be flatter and more flexible. Life will be unreasonable in the sense that it won't go on as it used to; we shall have to make things happen for us rather than wait for them to happen. What I had not anticipated, however, in that first book, was the confusion this would cause; that the opportunities for personal fulfillment which I so confidently predicted would be complicated by the pressures for efficiency, that the new freedoms would often mean less equality

and more misery, and that success might carry a disproportionate price.

One criticism of *The Age of Unreason,* that "it was all
very easy for people like you," had hit home. I am more
chary, now, of offering general solutions to our individual
predicaments. We must each find our own way. The
map, however, will be much the same for all of us, even if
we choose to follow different paths. In this book I offer
pointers to the future, challenges that I think will face all
organizations and all individuals, and some frameworks
for thinking about them, but this time there are no sure-
fire recipes for success.

One or two ideas which had their first exposure in
the last book have acquired a new significance for me.
The Inside-Out Doughnut is a metaphor that I used in
that book to describe the way jobs would be designed in
the future. That metaphor becomes, in this book, one of
the guiding principles of life in an age of paradox. It may
seem paradoxical, but I have found that one needs simple, homely, images to make sense of a complicated
world. Another concept which first surfaced in *The Age of
Unreason* was that of "portfolio," used there to describe
the new type of independent career. In this book I extend the concept into education because its imagery has
a wider application.

The important question is whether we shall all be
heading in the same general direction. Is there a point to
it all, and if so, what is it? Vaclav Havel, playwright
turned president, could hardly be more immersed in
worldly matters these days, but he has argued that we
will only avoid "mega-suicide" in our time if we rediscover a respect for something beyond ourselves. It is a
paradox, he says, but without that respect for a superper-

sonal moral order, we will not be able to create the social structures in which a person can truly be a person. We cannot be the measure of all things, perhaps, unless we have something against which to measure ourselves. I return to this issue in the last part of the book, but it lurks behind every page. The study of philosophy, I was once told, is the study of life, but don't expect it to tell you how to live. A bit like this book, I suspect.

In the Dark Wood

Confused by Paradox

1 *We Are Not Where We Hoped to Be*

IT DOESN'T
MAKE SENSE

There will be no one to pick the olives in parts of Italy this year. The old people are too old and the young will not do it for the money on offer. In Tuscany they did not bother to replace many of the olive groves destroyed in the harsh winter of 1985. It was not worth it. Now olive farming has to be a serious business, offering serious jobs for serious prices.

Changing, too, are those small family restaurants where the daughter helped her mother in the kitchen and the same waiter was there at lunchtime and in the evening, every day, every week. In most countries the law no longer allows jobs with hours like that, so that eating out is more expensive, like the olives, and many small restaurants are now uneconomic. "I'm really working for the government now," said the owner of one, "collecting their taxes and keeping unemployment down. There is nothing for me at the end of the day."

We have priced many jobs out of existence all over

the industrialized world. People need good wages to live in these countries. Governments need taxes. Not all products or services can carry these costs. Window cleaning does not merit a craftsman's wage, nor is a bottle of milk delivered to a British front door each morning really worth more than the price of a bottle of wine. Remove the subsidy and the delivery will end.

Proper jobs are now expensive jobs, providing high-priced goods and services for those who can afford such things. For the rest, it is do-it-yourself, grow your own olives, clean your own windows, or collect your own milk. Fair enough. Yet across a narrow strip of sea from those unpicked Italian olive trees live the Albanians, a desperately poor people who would be happy to pick olives or clean windows for a pittance. Every rich country has its neighboring Albanians. If we let them in to do the work no one else will do, someone else will have to pay for their lodging, their health care, and, ultimately, their old age. So we keep them out, mostly, if we can.

Many of them, however, already are here. They are our own citizens, but perhaps not qualified enough, not diligent enough, to be able to add enough value to cover their salaries. They are, literally, not worth employing in a proper job. Yet they are our citizens, with a right to a life, and, arguably, a right not only to a livelihood but to the sort of work that makes life worth living. They are also the customers for those who are producers. Keep them poor, as potential cheap labor when needed, and you bleed the market of demand. That, at present, seems to be the best we can do, offering bits and pieces of pocket-money work. America, in the years from 1973 to 1989, managed to create 32 million net new jobs compared with 5 million in the whole of Western Europe, but it was mostly hamburger work for hamburger pay.

It is one of the dilemmas of a rich society. There are more. Even those proper jobs are not unalloyed bliss. Much is demanded of those who have them. I asked a young friend, proud of his new job in a London bank, to come for a drink one evening. "I cannot get away until 9 p.m.," he said. "Not ever?" I asked. "Not really," he said, "my group expects me to be there until late, and on most Saturdays too. I can't let them down." It was exhilarating work, for the most part, he said, and very well paid, but it was totally consuming. His neglected partner said, "It's a crazy system. It doesn't make sense. Why don't they employ twice as many people at half the salary and work them half as hard? That way they could all lead a normal life."

But they don't, and they won't, and they can't, not if they want to remain competitive. A chairman of a large pharmaceutical company summed up his policy very neatly, but it was the other way round: "$1/2 \times 2 \times 3 = P$," he said, half as many people in the core of his business in five years' time, paid twice as well, and producing three times as much, that is what equals productivity and profit. Other businesses may not formulate it so crisply but that is the way they are all going: good jobs, expensive jobs, productive jobs, but many fewer of them. It makes good *corporate* sense.

These jobs are not for everyone. They are not for people who want more space in their lives for other things. For families, for instance. These kinds of jobs are difficult for women if they want to raise a family, or for men, for that matter, who might want to do likewise.

Child rearing can be delegated, of course, but it is not what everyone wants. "I insist that the company pay for me to read a bedtime story to my children on an international call when I'm away on business," said one account executive mother, but there is more to parenthood than telephoned bedtime stories.

Nor do they last forever, these jobs. We rightly deplore age discrimination in our society but 70-hour weeks are wearying. At some stage energy must yield to wisdom, or sometimes just to exhaustion. "Burnout" would not have become a popular word if there were nothing for it to describe. In many of these very full jobs we seem to be cramming the 100,000 hours of a traditional lifetime's work into 30 years instead of the traditional 47 years. Furthermore, do we really owe a job to a person who cannot really do it anymore? Behind those high salaries and big wages is the risk that you may, one day, not be worth it. Sometimes it seems that there is nothing so insecure as a secure job.

A 30-year job leaves 20 years or more "beyond the job" for nearly everyone, for if we have not died by the age of 50 we are unlikely to die before 75, unless we do something silly. Those 25 years cannot properly be called "retirement." They offer the possibility of another life for everyone. Jung believed that the first half of life is the preparation for the second half. Now that most of us will have the opportunity to use that second half in full measure we are strangely unprepared for it. Many of us waste it. "All I want is more of the same," said a friend. Unfortunately, that is seldom possible.

The dilemmas, and the paradoxes, continue. Akio Morita, chairman of Sony, noted that each Japanese worker put in an average of 2,159 hours in 1989. That compared with 1,546 hours for the average German. Other countries fell in between. The young Japanese, suggested Morita, will not long tolerate such a divergence, particularly the young, well-educated women who are now joining Japanese corporations. After all, the difference is equivalent to 15 40-hour weeks more than the Germans every year. No wonder the birth rate in Tokyo is now only 1.1 babies per female, half of what is needed to sustain the population. There is, literally, no time for babies *and* work. How, and when, these work patterns will change in such a country of tradition is anybody's guess, but if they do not change, Japan will have an increasingly resentful, aging, and diminishing workforce. Morita's remarks raised the eyebrows of Japan's elders, but, in a 1993 opinion poll, 87% of respondents agreed that they wanted the change.

For Germany, on the other hand, the challenge is to continue to make every hour a German works as effective as the one hour and 20 minutes put in by a worker in Japan. The Germans will need to do that in order to maintain their competitive position. It is a demanding standard, even if the Japanese begin to relax. It is a high standard, particularly for the now united Germany, where two different traditions of work still clash.

"Work," said a friend in Dresden, in the old East Germany, "used to be a place one went to, not something one did. We could not always work very productively because the parts or the tools we needed were not there. Anyway the customers were used to waiting and we got paid the same whether we did anything or not." I must have looked appalled because he went on, "I don't mean that it was right, or even sustainable as a system, but it did mean that there was a lot of time and energy for family and friends, for festivals and fun. Now," he smiled ruefully, "it seems to be all about profit and performance, pay, and productivity. Sometimes I think that I preferred the four 'f's to the four 'p's! What is it all about?"

We all share, to some degree, the dilemmas of both Japan and Germany. When we worked to ensure our own survival it was hard but understandable. Many people are now fortunate enough to be beyond survival. Today, "What now?" or "What next?" are the questions. Their answers are increasingly demanded of our political leaders, businesses, schools and hospitals and prisons, and, of course and most pressingly, of ourselves. One answer is to redefine survival. We can define it as keeping up with our neighbors, as individuals, as businesses, and as nations. But that answer has a no-win, nightmarish touch if we take it seriously. Only one firm can be the industry leader, only one country on top economically; there are always richer or more successful neighbors to compare ourselves with. Competition is healthy, maybe even essential, but there has to be more to life than winning or nearly all of us will be losers.

Maybe that is already happening. In 1992 the U.S. Congressional Budget Office, a scrupulously nonpartisan body, revealed that personal income in the United States, after adjustment for inflation, increased by $740 billion between 1977 and 1989. Of this total, almost two-thirds went to just 660,000 families, the wealthiest 1%. For that fortunate group, average income rose from $315,000 to $560,000, or by 77%. The middle classes gained a miserly 4% over this period, while 40% of all families actually ended up worse off in real terms at the end of this decade of affluence. The incentives, which may have been the fertilizers to grow more wealth, ended up consuming all the wealth they created.

While there are some arguments about the precise interpretation of these figures, it is clear that wealth did not trickle down too well in America during the Reagan years. Nor did it elsewhere. The figures for Britain are no different. A government report in 1993 revealed that for the period 1979–1990 the bottom 10% saw their income in real terms *fall* by 14%, while the average household income *increased* by 36%. The wealth was slightly less skewed in the other mature economies, but the trend was the same: the rich got richer and the poor got, relatively, poorer the world over, and sometimes poorer in absolute terms. What held it all together was only the hope among the poor that, maybe, in a world of constant growth there would be room for some of them amid the rich. That is beginning to seem a rather wistful, forlorn hope. Something is not working as it should.

Al Gore, before he became the vice president of the United States, wrote:

> We have constructed in our civilization a false world of plastic flowers and Astro-Turf, air-conditioning and fluorescent lights, windows that don't open and background music that never stops, days when we don't know whether it has rained, nights when the sky never stops glowing, Walkman and Watchman, entertainment cocoons, frozen food for the microwave oven, sleepy hearts jump-started by caffeine, alcohol, drugs and illusions.

He could have made it sound much worse had he described the wastelands of many inner cities. In these wastelands there are mindless murders of tiny children, rapes of old ladies, burglaries and thefts every 30 seconds in places, a total disregard for human life and property, senseless, anonymous violence.

Al Gore was writing out of concern for the environment. He could as well have been writing out of concern for the human spirit. That we have a spirit, most of us feel sure. We are not incidental curiosities, mutations in the evolutionary process. It would be a waste of our progress if we sacrificed that human spirit in the pursuit of some imagined efficiency.

Many things are not working too well just now. Even if we ignore, for a moment, the turbulent conflicts in the old Soviet empire, the endless dilemmas of the Middle East, the pitiless wars and famines of Africa, and our continued inability to save what is left of the global environment for our grandchildren, there are enough problems in what we thought were the successful capitalist nations to make us wonder if we missed the right road to the future. We are not where we had hoped to be at the end of this millennium.

UNINTENDED CONSEQUENCES OF "PROGRESS"

The millennium is only a statistical accident, but the close of a thousand years of history does concentrate the mind wonderfully, particularly when it seems to be coinciding with the disappearance of some things we have taken for granted for the past few generations, such as the employment organization.

Last Christmas the family game was to list all the things that had gotten better in the past decade. The intention was to bring a note of cheer into the proceedings. We all agreed on New Zealand wine and hospices, but got bogged down after that. Some championed CD Walkmans and some the personal phone but they hardly seemed to classify as advancing civilization. The game soon became too depressing to be fun.

Nevertheless, some things have gotten better. Because of what we have done in the past 50 years, almost everyone in industrialized societies has more things, more equipment, better health, and better housing. That is the good news. But these things have unintended costs, and when we look back, dispassionately, over that last half-century, the news is mixed. These were the years of my generation, the generation now moving slowly into their late middle age, the age beyond the organization and full-time responsibilities. It was this generation that set out to build a new world order after World War II which saw capitalism triumph over communism and which kept muzzled the ogre of nuclear war. Some things, however, we did not foresee.

It was this generation that used technology to make a dramatic improvement in productivity, but thought too little about those who would no longer be required to perform the old essential tasks. What work there will be in the future will, for many, be nonessential work, selling goods and services that we could happily do without, building yellow-page economies of glitz and extras, hardly the stuff of real life. Many will not even have this sort of work. This was not intended.

The reward of productivity was increased consumption. To be a customer was seen as the new enlightenment. Even Britain's much-vaunted Citizen's Charter turned out, on inspection, to be a customer's charter. We did not realize soon enough that too much consumption has its costs, that the freedom to drive a car, for instance, all too often ends up as freedom to sit in a traffic jam, or that the delights of tourism dwindle when everyone you meet is also a tourist. We made consumption a measure of achievement, unwittingly creating a society of envy, in which to be poor means having less than the average, even if the average is quite high. This is a no-win world, and unintended.

We misinterpreted Adam Smith's ideas to mean that if we each looked after our own interests, some "invisible hand" would mysteriously arrange things so that it all worked out for the best for all. We therefore promulgated the rights of the individual and freedom of choice for all. But without self-restraint, without thought for one's neighbor and one's grandchildren, such freedom becomes license and mere selfishness. Adam Smith, who was a professor of Moral Philosophy, not of Economics, built his theories on the basis of a moral community. Before he wrote *The Wealth of Nations* he had written his definitive work, *A Theory of Moral Sentiments,* arguing that a stable society was based on "sympathy," a moral duty to have regard for your fellow human beings. The market is a mechanism for sorting the efficient from the inefficient, it is not a substitute for responsibility.

As a result of all the "progress" of the past 50 years, many have done well, but many not so well, even in the rich societies. In the world at large, the rich still get richer and the poor get poorer in spite of our best intentions. The road we have been on, throughout this century, has been the road of management, planning, and control. Those who stood on top of society's mountains could most clearly see the way ahead; they could, and should, plan the route for the rest and make sure that they followed it. In many ways the bigger the mountain, we thought, the better and clearer the view. We applied this approach to our organizations. We thought this way about government; even when we said that government should get off the backs of the people we did not really mean it because then people would not be managed to their best advantage. We have tried to plan and control world trade and world finance and to make a greener world. There should be a rational response to everything, we thought; it should be possible to make a better world.

It hasn't worked. Management and control are breaking down everywhere. The new world order looks very likely to end in disorder. We can't make things happen the way we want them to at home, at work, or in government, certainly not in the world as a whole. There are, it is now clear, limits to management. We thought that capitalism was the answer, but some of the hungry and homeless might not agree.

THE INEVITABILITY
OF PARADOX

We need a new way of thinking about our problems and our futures. My suggestion is the management of paradox, an idea which is itself a paradox, in that paradox can only be "managed" in the sense of coping with. Manage always did mean "coping with," until we purloined the word to mean planning and control.

I used to think that paradoxes were the visible signs of an imperfect world, a world which would, one day, be better understood and better organized. There had to be one right way to bring up children, I thought. There should be no reason for some people to starve while others gorge. Freedom need not mean license, violence, or even war. Riches for some do not necessarily imply poverty for others. We lacked only the knowledge and the will to resolve such paradoxes. We did not yet know enough about how things worked, I thought, but eventually there would be what scientists call "A Theory of Everything," and, as Stephen Hawking, the Cambridge physicist, put it, probably ironically, we would then know the mind of God. In my own sphere, I wrote books that implied that there had to be a right way to run our organizations and our lives, even if we could not yet be completely sure of what it was. I was in the grip of the idea that everything, in theory, could be understood, predicted, and, therefore, managed.

I no longer believe in A Theory of Everything, or in the possibility of perfection. Paradox I now see to be inevitable, endemic, and perpetual. The more turbulent the times, the more complex the world, the more paradoxes there are. We can, and should, reduce the starkness of some of the contradictions, minimize the inconsistencies, understand the puzzles in the paradoxes, but we cannot make them disappear, or solve them completely, or escape from them. Paradoxes are like the weather, something to be lived with, not solved, the worst aspects mitigated, the best enjoyed and used as clues to the way forward. Paradox has to be *accepted,* coped with, and made sense of, in life, in work, in the community, and among nations.

There was a small, framed, printed motto which hung in my boyhood bedroom: "Life goes, you see, to golf's own ditty; Without the rough there'ld be no pretty." I have no idea why it was there. My family did not go in for such things and my mother had probably picked it up at a charity bazaar. Accidental or not, it was my first subliminal introduction to the necessity of paradox in human affairs. As I grew older, I realized that what I had been told was God's great gift to mankind—choice—turned out to be itself a paradox because the freedom to choose implies the freedom to choose wrong, to sin. You cannot have the one without the other. Sin, original sin, therefore, is the price we pay for our humanity. There was paradox at the heart of religion. Quite right, too, I came to realize, because paradox is what makes life interesting. If everything was an unmixed blessing, life would soon begin to cloy. There would be no need for change or movement. Offer me a heaven without paradox and I will opt for hell. Perfection, then, is neither possible nor, perhaps, desirable.

For me that conclusion was a revelation. There is paradox at the heart of things. Life will never be easy, or perfectible, or completely predictable. It will be best understood backward, but we have to live it forward. To make it livable at all levels we have to learn to use the paradoxes—to balance contradictions and inconsistencies—as an invitation to find a better way. F. Scott Fitzgerald once said that the test of a first-class mind was the ability to hold two opposing ideas in the head at the

THE WILL OF GOD IS EASY TO UNDERSTAND IN RETROSPECT

same time and still retain the ability to function. If he was right, we are in trouble, because there are not that many first-class minds around. Schumacher, in *Small Is Beautiful*, also put it well: "[Some people] always tend to clamour for a final solution, as if in life there could ever be a final solution other than death. For constructive work, the principal task is always the restoration of some kind of balance."

Living with paradox is not comfortable or easy. It can be like walking in a dark wood on a moonless night. It is an eerie and, at times, a frightening experience. All sense of direction is lost; trees and bushes crowd in on you; wherever you step, you bump into another obstacle; every noise and rustle is magnified; there is a whiff of danger; it seems safer to stand still than to move. Come the dawn, however, and your path is clear; the noises are now the songs of birds and the rustle in the undergrowth is only scuttling rabbits; trees define the path instead of blocking it. The wood is a different place. So will our world look different and less frightening if we can bring light to the paradoxes.

PROPHETS AND KINGS

"There are kings and prophets, I was always told," said Tony Benn, the British socialist politician. "The kings have the power and the prophets have the principles." I am on the side of the kings, the people who make things happen, but every king needs his prophet to help him, and increasingly her, keep a clear head amidst the confusions. No one, however, would want the prophet to run the show.

Prophets, in spite of their name, do not foretell the future. No one can do that, and no one should claim to do so. What prophets can do is to tell the truth as they see it. They can point to the emperor's lack of clothes, that things are not what people like to think they are. They can warn of dangers ahead if the course is not changed. They can, and often do, point to what they think to be wrong, unjust, or prejudiced. Most of all, they can offer a way to clarify the dilemmas and concentrate the mind.

What the prophet cannot, and should not, do is to tell the doers what to do. That would be taking the power without the responsibility, the prerogative of the harlot, they used to say, not the prophet. The prophet can provide a chart but cannot dictate where or how the vessel should sail. It is that chart which I aim to provide in this book.

It is my hope that such a chart will make it easier for people to see a way through the confusions of our times. Some of those people will be the leaders and executives of our institutions, because, in what I see as the ending of the age of the organization, those institutions will have very different futures. Yet, in their new forms, they will be more essential than ever.

Some of the people reading this book will be individuals trying to make sense of their lives. Young people, in particular, face a world very different from the one their parents grew up in, a world where they really do have to re-invent their lives, their purposes, their standards, and their priorities.

Finally, I would like to think that the ideas and thoughts in the book might be useful to those responsible for the governance of our society, at all levels. They have the awesome responsibility of finding a structure for a society where most of the ground rules have changed but where the need for justice between groups, and between the present and the future, is greater than ever.

We need a new perspective on life, on its purpose and its responsibilities. There are few great causes or crusades anymore. Maybe it is the end of history. Some people are cocooned in comfort, others in poverty; but for either group, survival seems to be the point of life. If that is so, we shall all lose in the end. If anything is to happen, however, it has to start with us, individually, in our own place and time. To wait for a leader to guide us into the future is to be forever disillusioned.

2 The Paradoxes of Our Times

Tales of confusion do little to help. If we are to cope with the turbulence of life today, we must start by organizing it in our minds. Until we do, we will feel impotent, victims of events beyond our control or even our capacity to understand. Framing the confusion is the first step to doing something about it. Analysts and therapists know this, of course, but so do the teachers of managers and doctors. The management students at my business school regularly discuss 30-page case studies, descriptions of the state of play in a business or an industry. Cases are not a facile attempt to give students an illusion of reality, but a way of teaching them that the first thing to do when confronted with a lot of data, impressions, and confusing signals is to put them into some sort of framework, as a doctor learns to turn symptoms into a diagnosis. Only then can treatment begin.

What follows is one way of framing our confusions, in the hope that we can begin to turn the turbulence into creation. I have identified nine principal paradoxes, nine ways of explaining what is going on in our societies and why some confusion is inevitable. There are obviously many more, for paradox has always been part of life. "That life succeeds in that it seems to fail," said Robert Browning, "is a paradox which comforts while it mocks." That quote is a fine example of the ironic aspect of paradox, the unexpected twist in so much of what we do. Simultaneous opposites are the other feature of paradox, as when, at times, we find that we can, at times, dislike those whom we love the most, but go on both loving and disliking. Paradox does not have to be resolved, only managed.

These nine paradoxes are far from an exhaustive list, but if we can manage them to forge a better world, we shall have done well. They are the paradoxes of mature economies. Not all of them are yet to be found, for instance, in Southeast Asia, still less in Africa. But their time will come, for these paradoxes seem to go hand in hand with economic progress everywhere.

1. The Paradox of Intelligence

For a long time, corporate chairmen have been saying that their real assets are their employees, but few of them really mean it and none have gone so far as to put those assets on their balance sheets. That may change. Peter Drucker points out that the "means of production," the traditional basis of capitalism, are now literally owned by the workers because those means are in their heads and at their fingertips. What Marx once dreamed of has become a reality, but in a way which he could never have imagined.

Intelligence has become the new form of property. Focused intelligence, the ability to acquire and apply knowledge and know-how, is the new source of wealth. Singapore, which calls itself The Intelligent Island, recognizes that the traditional sources of wealth and comparative advantage—land, raw materials, money, and technology—can all be bought when and if needed, *provided* one has the people with the intelligence and the know-how to apply them. Singapore, along with Hong Kong, has exported all its manufacturing activities to cheaper places like Sumatra, the Philippines, and Guangdong in China, but retains managerial control, design, and distribution—the intelligence quotient.

What is true for Singapore is true everywhere. The new source of wealth in our societies is the intelligence quotient. Intelligence is, therefore, the new form of property. Unfortunately intelligence does not behave like any other form of property, and therein lies the paradox. It is, for instance, impossible to give people intelligence by decree or to redistribute it. It is not even possible to leave it to your children when you die. Of course, there is education—which becomes the crucial key to future wealth—but it is a key which takes a long time to shape and a long time to turn. The situation gets odder. Even if I do manage to share my intelligence or know-how with you, I still keep it all. It is not possible to take this new form of property away from anyone. Intelligence is sticky.

Nor is it possible to own someone else's intelligence. Peter Drucker is right—the means of production can, in practice, no longer be owned by the people who think they own the business. It is hard to prevent brains from walking out of the door if they want to. Buying shares in a company like Microsoft is a bet that the intelligence of its workers will continue to be exercised on the firm's behalf and that the intelligence never flags. Intelligence is an insecure basis for the stock market. It is a leaky form of property.

An added complication is that intelligence is extraordinarily difficult to measure, which is why intellectual property seldom appears on balance sheets. But this also makes it difficult to tax, unlike any other form of property, which in turn makes any form of wealth or property taxation ineffective. Intelligence is tricky, as well as sticky and leaky.

The good news is that, while it is impossible to redistribute intelligence by administrative fiat, it is also impossible to stop people from getting it. In theory, anyone can be intelligent in some way or can become intelligent and thereby have access to power and wealth. There is little to stop a small firm muscling in on Microsoft's territory just as Microsoft did to IBM. When the key property is intelligence, you do not have to be big or rich to get in on the act. It is a low-cost entry marketplace. It should make for a more open society.

Unfortunately, intelligence tends to go where intelligence is. Well-educated people give their children a good education, which gives them access to power and wealth. The most likely outcome of the new form of property, therefore, is an increasingly divided society, unless we can transform the whole of society into a permanent learning culture where everyone pursues a higher intelligence quotient as avidly as they now look for a home of their own. A property-owning democracy on this basis is an exciting thought.

As a small indicator of the changing perception of property, we may observe that the richer we are, the less need we seem to feel to own our own homes. In Bangladesh over 90% of houses are owner-occupied; in Ireland,

82%. In rich Germany, the western part, the figure falls to 45%. In richer Switzerland it is only 33%. Where brains prevail, security lies not in physical property but in the intelligence quotient. There are, then, better uses for cash than buying houses.

2. The Paradox of Work

We all need something to do. Activity is natural. It is hard to see why there should be a shortage of it, yet enforced idleness seems to be the price we pay for improved efficiency. Why should we worry? To be pleasurably idle was the dream of the ancients, their concept of civilization. "If work were so great," quipped Mark Twain, "the rich would have hogged it long ago." They have, Mr. Twain, they have. The result is that some people have work and money but too little leisure time, while others have all the leisure time but no work and no money. Those who are idle do not see it as a privilege but as a curse because they tend to be at the bottom of the heap. We seem to have made work into a god and then made it difficult for many to worship.

Why has work become so lumpy? Part of the problem is money. Work is society's chosen way of distributing income. We will do even boring work for the money it brings. Therefore it would be convenient if everyone had some work to do, even if it was boring, as a way of getting the money to them. This was part of the communist philosophy. Unfortunately, we also use money as the measure of efficiency. Our organizations want the most work for the least money while individuals typically want the most money for the least work. In a competitive world, it is not hard to see that the organization is going to win.

Organizations are tackling the challenge of efficiency by exporting unproductive work, and people, as fast as they can. Instead of keeping a pool of slightly surplus labor and skills inside the organization as a cushion for emergencies and comfort, they are pushing those skills outside and pulling them in when necessary. If you approve of this approach you call it "getting rid of slack"; if you disapprove, you talk of "exporting their flexibility onto the peripheral labor market." Put many of the full-time workers outside and it is they, not the organization, who will bear the costs of their unused time. Slack always costs money. It is only a question of who pays for it.

The irony is that these unused workers still have to have some money if they are to live and to enjoy some of the rights and pleasures of citizenship. The money has, ultimately, to come in some way from the organizations they left, usually in the form of higher taxes. In the end, much the same work gets done, for the total output of the economy has not risen that much, and much the same money gets paid out, but in different ways. Odd, isn't it? In theory it need not happen this way. In theory, those spare workers with spare time will invent new work to keep themselves busy and in cash. Unfortunately, they are usually the people least capable of creating new work for themselves because they lack the kinds of intelligence and inclinations that would allow them to be independent. (Having conditioned them to life as employees, we now expect them to be entrepreneurs.)

To herald the new year in 1993, Burton, a British chain of clothing shops, announced it would cut 2,000 full-time jobs but create 3,000 part-time ones. It was, Burton said, a strategic response to the stretched day and the stretched week of modern retailing. The company was not typical. It is no wonder, then, that only 55% of Britain's workforce now has full-time employment. There is a lot of spare capacity in the economy these days, but it is in individuals, not organizations. It is not clear how we unlock that capacity, except by giving these outsiders a share in the intelligence quotient. Until we do, re-lumping the work so that some have too much and some too little will only divide society.

In fact, Britain and the United States have the most open labor markets and, therefore, the highest number of people at work—but their workers are the least protected and often the worst paid. Some 70% of working-age Americans and Britons have paid work. That compares with 60% in France and only 50% in Spain. As we noted earlier, America created 32 million new jobs in the 16 years from 1973 to 1989 compared with 5 million for Europe as a whole. BUT the Americans and the British have to work longer and odder hours, accept more part-time and self-employment, and enjoy less protection. Fifteen percent of British workers put in more than 48 hours a week and 20% regularly work on Sundays. The continentals think this is mad. Britain and America add on less than 30% to wages or salaries to take care of social security and pensions. Italy, France, and Germany add 50%. Should you have fewer, better-paid, better-educated, and better-protected workers, or more but cheaper ones? The continental Europeans argue that only good, and therefore expensive, labor is worthwhile in this modern age, and that no work is better than bad work, while the British and Americans believe that any work is better than no work, even if the result is a progressively downskilled workforce. One consequence of the British and American view is a more divided society. In America the top 10% of earners are paid six times as much as the bottom 10%. In Germany the ratio is just over two. We need a way through this paradox.

The way may be a redefinition of work. Work is more than a job. There are more forms of activity than paid work. Indeed, if work is priced at zero, there is unlimited scope for it. "I know that only too well," my housewife friends respond. "If we were paid for what we do, much of what we do would not be worth doing; we could not afford the price of a clean house or an evening meal if that price had to include our reasonable wages." Therefore, if people want work for reasons other than money—self-respect or identity, to make a contribution, or to feel part of something—the answer is to price more work at zero. In a society like China where a lot of the work is not priced, everyone is busy. Ironically, the more you price work, the less paid work gets done because so much of it is not worth the cost. Any work that is worth its price is quickly turned into a business, where the few are paid well and the many not, because that way efficiency lies. Perhaps we should be pricing work high, or at zero, rather than fiddling around in between. That, however, leads to the next paradox.

3. The Paradox of Productivity

Productivity means more and better work from fewer people. That is good for the customer and good for the organization, be it a business or a public service. No one has ever been against efficiency. It has, generally, been good, also, for the workers, even those who are not included in the "fewer." The ones who stayed got better jobs, and better-paid ones. Those who left found work in other growing organizations. Over time they moved into the new growth sectors of the economy. Thus it was that two hundred years ago agricultural workers began to find new work in the new factories, and their descendants, when factories started slimming and closing, moved to the offices and shops of the service sector. Growth, and work, went on. As long as the overall growth rate was at least equal to the rate of improvement in efficiency, plus the rate of growth of the population, there would always be a job somewhere for everyone.

This time, however, the new growth sector for work is the do-it-yourself economy, and therein lies the new paradox. Some of that do-it-yourself economy is paid for and counted because the self-employment sector is growing everywhere; some of it is paid for but not counted—the black economy; some is the purely destructive do-it-yourself world of crime and violence. Much of this do-it-yourself economy is, however, neither paid for nor counted nor illegal—when we look after our old and sick, do our own repairs, grow our own food. As more and more people get pushed out of or leave organizations, it makes good economic sense for them to do for themselves what they used to pay others to do. Logically, they should go in for a little personal import substitution, something every government advocates as desirable nationally, but would rather we did not do individually and domestically. Why pay other people to do or make what you can do or make yourself if, now, you have more time than money? Because this new growth sector is invisible, productivity this time around does not seem to be producing the output increases, nor the conventional jobs, which we would have expected.

This is not a temporary paradox, governments and the unemployed please note. Society, and individuals, will have to get used to the do-it-yourself economy as the new growth sector. More of us are going to be in it whether we like it or not. Better technology means that more and more of us can run businesses or services by ourselves. More of us will be outside the organization and the formal economy. The OECD calculated that, in 1992, only 33% of the British aged over 55 were in paid work. Before you write that off as a British peculiarity, you should know that the figure for France was 27% and for Italy 11%. The rest were not all doing nothing, but what they were doing was not counted, statistically or, more crucially, socially.

Economies have traditionally grown, in measured economic terms, by turning unpriced work into priced work because that work can be counted. The irony is that, although the economy appears to grow, the work that is done may actually be reduced. By pricing the work, we turn "activity" into "jobs" and create employment, but then some work gets too expensive for the customers to afford and so no longer gets done. In many cases, we can't do it ourselves for free because we have forgotten how to do it. The activity disappears. By pricing work we can destroy work, but we will never notice it because it never got counted in the first place.

Besides having a paid job, a friend of mine used to grow all his own vegetables, even producing his own seeds; it was a source of pride to him that he ate for free. The visible economy was the poorer for it because nothing was bought or sold. As he grew older and richer, however, he calculated that growing vegetables was a poor use of his time. He would be better off spending more time on his own work and buying the vegetables in the supermarket. The visible economy grew a notch or two thereby. But my friend lost his job and could no longer afford to buy any but the cheapest vegetables. Unfortunately by this time he had disposed of his vegetable plot and tools. He had no energy to start over again. He was bored, poor, and hungry. The economy had slipped back a notch again, but now less vegetables in total were being consumed in that house, there was more idleness and more dissatisfaction. By pricing his work my friend had ultimately destroyed it.

His story is a parable of the rich societies that by pricing work have increasingly drawn more types of work into their formal economies. They have encouraged specialization and efficiency but, as a result, have priced some of that new work out of existence, de-skilled many of their citizens, and created a class of people who have nothing to do if they have no job. All of these consequences are a result of good intentions, a downside of progress, but reveal one of the more uncomfortable paradoxes of modern times.

4. The Paradox of Time

In this turbulent world we never seem to have enough time, yet there has never been so much time available to us. We live longer, use less time to make and do things as we become more efficient, and should therefore have more time to spare. We have, however, made this strange commodity into a competitive weapon, paying over the odds for speed. If we were wise shouldn't we take the price tag off time, and give ourselves time to stand and stare?

There was a time when we knew what time was. Patricia Hewitt, of Britain's Institute of Public Policy Research, put it neatly—the time that men spent on paid employment determined how much time they had for their families; the time women spent caring for their families determined how much time they had for work. Most men spent most of their time in or around organizations, most women spent most of their time working in the home. Organizations, you might say, were organized for male convenience, but, as a result, time was more or less fixed. We all knew who was where and when.

I have been using the past tense. Only one-third of British workers now work the "normal" 9 to 5 day, give or take an hour or two at each end. The normal is now the minority. Time is coming unfixed. Organizations want more flexibility. We have to re-think time and the words that we have attached to time. I can see a future when it will no longer be possible to draw a hard distinction between full- and part-time work, when "retirement" will be a purely technical term, signaling an entitlement to financial benefits, and when "overtime" as a concept will seem as outmoded as "servant" does today. At present, however, time is more unbalanced than balanced for many, which means that their lives are also out of balance. Some have more time than they know what to do with, while others have too little time to do all they want to.

Organizations are now re-thinking time for their own advantage, as if they had finally realized that there are actually 168 hours in the week, not 40. Sleeping assets make no money, so why shut them down for 128 hours a week when half of the world is still awake, when customers like to shop at the end of the day and the end of the week, and when some people like to work while others sleep. Most factories are now like process plants, working a 24-hour day. There are night shifts in financial offices worldwide, stores in London that stay open until 9 p.m. or 10 p.m. and on Sundays. Schools in Wandsworth in South London have abandoned the long summer holiday, originally designed to allow pupils to help with the harvest, in favor of five eight-week terms. Time demarcations are not sacrosanct anymore.

There is a long list of the ways in which organizations are re-chunking time. There is flextime, which has been with us for a while, but if we moved to a 35-hour week, flextime could mean an hour off each working day, or Friday afternoons off, or a nine-day fortnight. And there is part-time work for new parents, part-time before retirement, job-sharing, term-time jobs, weekend jobs, four ten-hour days a week or eight-day fortnights, annual hours contracts, zero-hour contracts (being available as and when required), parental leave, career breaks, sabbaticals, time-banking (accumulating vacation time over several years), and individual hour contracts where individuals and their bosses agree on a timetable of hours per week or month.

On the face of it, there is enough flexibility for everyone. Why, then, does Juliet Schor need to write a book called *The Overworked American,* which sells so well that it must have struck a chord with many? The average American, she finds, now works 164 more hours per year than 20 years ago—the equivalent of an extra month. The typical American now works 47 hours per week, and if current trends continue, in 20 years he or she will be on the job 60 hours a week, for an annual total of 3,000 hours. That compares with 1,856 hours per week in Britain in 1989. Why do they do it? Schor says that organizations want fewer people working longer because it saves on overhead, while individuals want the money. This "Faustian bargain of time for money," says Schor, has created an insidious cycle of work and spend as people increasingly look to consumption to give satisfaction and even meaning to their lives.

The paradox is that they seem to know that it is stupid. In a U.S. Department of Labor survey in 1978, 84% of the respondents said that they would choose to trade off some future increases in income for more leisure time, with almost half opting to trade *all* the increases. In Britain, Andre Gortz told of overtime-loving workers at a shoe factory. When hard times hit, the factory went into work-sharing, and the employees who had worked all the extra hours they could get, including Sundays and holidays, found themselves with time on their hands. One worker reported: "Bit by bit, there was an unbelievable phenomenon of physical recuperation. The idea of money really lost its intensity. It's quite true that we lost a good deal of money [25% of previous income] but, quite soon, only one or two of the blokes minded. It was about now that . . . friendships began: we were now able to go beyond political conversation, and we managed to talk about love, impotence, jealousy, family life . . . it was also at this time that we realized the full horror of working in the factory on Saturday afternoon or evenings . . . we were once again learning the meaning of living."

Schor says that Americans seem to have decided to take the benefits of the improved productivity of the past 50 years in money rather than time. Work and spend has become a habit. She is the first to recognize, of course, that for some people there is no choice. Nearly one-third of American workers earn wages that, on a full-time basis, would not lift them out of poverty. The same is true of Britain. Millions of people can only make ends meet through overtime, moonlighting, or multi-earning households. They would willingly give more time to make more money just to make ends meet.

The trouble started when we turned time into a commodity, when we bought people's time in our organizations rather than buying their produce. Under these conditions, the more time you sell, the more money you make. There is an inevitable trade-off between time and money. Organizations, for their part, get choosy. They want less time from the people they pay by the hour but more from the people they pay by the year because, in the latter case, every extra hour during the year is free.

Time turns out to be a confusing commodity. Some people will spend money to save their time, others will spend their time to save money and others will trade money for time at certain periods of their life, preferring to work less for less money. This makes time a contradictory sort of commodity, but one that will become more and more important in our societies.

Busy people will, if they can afford it, spend money to save time, buying time-saving equipment for their homes, pre-cooked meals, and help with their chores; they will prefer taxis to buses, child minders to child minding, gardeners to gardening if it allows them to spend their time on what they really want to do. Their needs create an important market opportunity. The affluent unbusy, on the other hand, spend money to buy time—time to travel, time to learn, time to play, and time to keep fit—or they spend their time doing themselves what they used to pay others to do. Time, therefore, creates the new growth area. Personal services for the busy, to save time; health, education, travel, and recreation for the affluent unbusy, to spend time; equipment and materials for those who want to spend time to save money. It is, perhaps, no accident that these new growth areas will not be best served by large corporations but by small independents providing personal and local delivery, linked perhaps by franchising or other networks into bigger combinations.

5. The Paradox of Riches

Economic growth depends, ultimately, on more and more people wanting more and more of more and more things. Looking at the world as a whole, then, there should be no shortage of growth potential. If, however, we look only at the rich societies, we see people having fewer babies every year and living longer. Eventually, fewer babies mean fewer customers, while longer lives mean, usually, poorer and more choosy customers. Older people, even when they have the money, are in a slimming-down, passing-on stage, not a stocking-up one. At home we could be running out of customers.

But not abroad, not, anyway, in the multiplying needy areas of the developing world. Their citizens, however, cannot afford to buy most of the things we have to sell. What they want are the know-how and the capital to make things to sell to us, before they can start to buy from us. Therefore, we will have to invest in our potential competitors in order to fuel our own growth. No government has been able to persuade its people to accept that paradox, although multinational businesses are beginning to see the sense, for their shareholders, of making things where they are cheaper, wherever that is, and exporting their know-how to make that possible. In the short term, however, exporting factories, and know-how not products, is nothing but bad news for those who used to work in those factories. It is their children who will benefit from a richer world outside, not them. Will they be prepared to make the sacrifice?

Back home, the traditional answer has been to create even more demand among those who have the money. Growth has to be fuelled by what the American economist Thorstein Veblen first called "conspicuous consumption" 100 years ago, the need to keep up with or be better than the neighbors. Growth, then, which is necessary for society, is increasingly dependent on a climate of envy in that society, increasing its divisions further. Paradox again. There are, however, some signs that the "Gucci factor" may have peaked in the 1980s, along with the firm of that name. It is, said the *Financial Times,* "the demise of de luxe." Couture houses in Paris are worried that no one will want to pay the prices for their creations. Consumers have become more discerning, less interested in conspicuous consumption, asking more often "Will it work well?" or "Will it last?" We have, paradoxically, to wonder whether this is good news or bad. It is bad for growth, good for common sense.

We shall miss one customer, the defense industries of the West. Politically legitimate, the defense industry created a demand for advanced technology which spread knowledge and work throughout the economies of America, Britain, and most Western countries. In yet another paradox, one must hope that this particular cus-

tomer will never again be needed to the same extent. For
the good of our economies, however, an alternative, and
politically legitimate, customer would be very beneficial.
We could, for instance, define the environment as a substitute for defense expenditure, fending off our own deteri-
oration. Sadly, turning swords into ploughshares has
never proved easy. Peace dividends quickly disappear
into the national loan account.

6. The Paradox of Organizations

We used to think that we knew how to run organizations.
Now we know better. More than ever they need to be
global and local at the same time, to be small in some
ways but big in others, to be centralized some of the time
and decentralized most of it. They expect their workers
to be both more autonomous and more of a team, their
managers to be more delegating and more controlling.
The paradox is neatly summed up in Charles Savage's
story, in his book *Fifth Generation Management,* of the manager saying to the new recruit, "The good news is that
you have 120,000 people working for you, the bad news
is that they don't know it."

John Stopford and Charles Baden-Fuller, in their
study of rejuvenating businesses, report that the successful ones live with paradox, or what they call "dilemmas."
Those firms have to be planned yet flexible, be differenti-
ated and integrated at the same time, be mass marketers
while catering to many niches; they must introduce new
technology but allow their workers to be masters of their
own destiny; they must find ways to produce variety and
quality and fashion, all at low cost; in short, they have to

reconcile what used to be opposites, instead of choosing between them.

Charles Hampden-Turner, in his book on corporate culture, also focuses on the inevitable dilemmas of organizations, arguing that managers have to be "masters of paradox," turning the horns of the dilemmas into virtuous, not vicious, circles. As an example, he quotes the Berkeley consultants, Meridian, who use the mythical Greek image of Scylla, the rock, and Charybdis, the whirlpool, which Odysseus and his sailors had to steer between, to characterize the hard and soft features of organizations, the structured, controlled, masculine side and the flexible, responsive, feminine side, both of which are needed for success.

These authors speak as if we would know this organization when we saw it, full of paradox though it may be. The organizations of the future may not be readily recognizable as such. When intelligence is its primary asset, the organization becomes more like a collection of project groups, some fairly permanent, some temporary, some in alliance with other parties. Instead of being a castle, a home for life for its defenders, an organization will be more like an apartment block, an association of temporary residents gathered together for mutual convenience. The apartment block may, in fact, not have a physical existence, because the project groups or clusters do not have to be in the same place or even employed by the same organization. Some companies are no more than temporary project groups, put together from various sources with a specific task to do, meeting mostly by video conferences and voice mail. This concept has led some people to talk of the "virtual corporation," something that can be discerned more easily on the computer screen than in the physical world. A corporation is nothing more than "a nexus of contracts" says Oliver Williamson of Berkeley. The challenge for tomorrow's leaders is to manage an organization that is not there in any sense in which we are used to.

It is, however, a challenge that must be met, because these minimalist, partly unseen, organizations are the linchpins of our world. Most of us may not belong to them, but we shall be selling our services to them, the wealth of our societies will depend upon them; ultimately, they will be the source of our well-being. The age of the organization may be coming to an end in the sense that being a full-time employee is a minority occupation, and that even for this minority the time spent in the organization represents less than half of one's adult life; but in another sense the organization, or what is left of it, will be the critical component of society. Organizations will organize, but to do so they will no longer need to employ. An organizing organization will look and feel very different from an employment organization. Because it will be less visible as an organization we should not think it is less important.

7. The Paradox of Aging

We all age, but each generation ages differently. This is technically called the "cohort factor." Each cohort or generation is affected by its own history. Therefore, it is unlikely that my children will have the same sort of life cycle that I have had, or that mine is like my parents'. My parents' generation lived through a world war, in some cases two of them. They went through a long and deep recession in the 1930s. They valued security above all else and they expected to, and did, work until almost the end of their lives.

It isn't the same anymore. Work inside organizations has petered out for many in their fifties, creating the kind of mid-life crisis for many which their parents had never known. Change speeded up. The world got smaller. Children did not die as often and were not killed in wars so we planned for smaller families. Divorce replaced death as the end of many a marriage, creating the kind of spread-eagled families which, to our parents, were a rarity. The problems we encountered were new; the crises were different. Society, however, was still geared to the aging patterns of the previous generation. Pension schemes, divorce laws, social expectations became inappropriate and took time to change.

It will happen again. My children, unlike previous cohorts, will find conventional jobs and careers harder to get. Their work lives will start later and end earlier, creating a gap between adolescence and adulthood which their parents never knew, a gap which many do not really know how to fill. Their relationships will be different from ours. Because they have grown up without wars, they will be more carefree with their plans and lives. Their education will have to be more prolonged, if not indefinite. All women will do paid work for most of their lives but both sexes may want, and need, to find intervals for child rearing and learning. Children are now a decision, not an accident. The roles of the sexes will change, and that change will bring different values and priorities.

The paradox of aging is that every generation perceives itself as justifiably different from its predecessor, but plans as if its successor generation will be the same. This time it needs to be different.

8. The Paradox of the Individual

Society speaks with two voices. One voice urges us to discover our "authentic self," to plan our own path through life and, while respecting the rights of others, to hold fast to the right to be ourselves. Individualism acquired a bad name in the years of Reagan and Thatcher, when, masquerading as "enterprise," it was used to justify the uninhibited pursuit of private gain. There was once, however, a more honorable British tradition, drawing on Darwin's idea of self-reliance and a rich tradition of eccentrics and opinion leaders. It was then, and is now again, respectable and desirable to be yourself.

The other voice is that of the receptionist or the conference organizer. "Whom do you represent?" "With whom are you affiliated?" "What organization are you from?" Recounting his problem with receptionists and switchboards, the British writer Anthony Sampson, who works from his own home, says, "I'm tempted to reply that I represent the human race . . . the inalienable right to life, liberty and the pursuit of happiness, but it won't get me through the switchboard. I have to reply that I represent no one or that 'I'm just a friend.' I feel even more freakish at conferences where everyone else seems to represent some company, organization or group." It was, he points out, John D. Rockefeller, the creator of Standard Oil, the first modern corporation, who remarked, "The day of combination is here to stay. Individualism has gone, never to return." Rockefeller was only partly right. An MIT study comparing American and Japanese working methods concluded that American workers had to balance their individualism with team work if they were to match the productivity of the Japanese. The Japanese, however, are looking for some of that individualism and creativity to balance the conforming force of their combinations.

It is a paradox, one best captured by Jung who said, years ago, that we need others to be truly ourselves. "I" needs "we" to be fully "I." Looking up, however, at the office blocks in every city, those little boxes piled on top of one another up into the sky, one has to wonder how much room there is for "I" amid the filing cabinets and the terminals. It was A.E. Housman, Sampson reminds us, who said in one of his poems, "I, a stranger and afraid, in a world I never made." Who will be the "we" to whom we would want to belong? Is it the minimalist, virtual organization? Or the "edge city" in suburbia? Or the disappearing family? Can a personal network substitute for these bonds?

9. The Paradox of Justice

Justice is the bond of society. We are happy to belong to a society that treats us fairly, that gives us our due and that is impartial. The problem is that "giving each their due" can mean a variety of contradictory things. It can, for instance, mean giving us what we deserve, be that a reward for achievement or a punishment for offenses. On the other hand it can mean giving us what we need. Political parties will champion one definition or the other and claim to be the party of justice. Both will be right.

Michael Young, 30 years ago, summed up the dilemmas of distributive justice very nicely:

> One could say that it was wrong to pay one man more than another because there should be distribution ac-

cording to needs. One could say that it was wrong to pay the lazy scientist more than the diligent dustman because there should be distribution according to effort. One could say that it was wrong to pay the intelligent more than the stupid because society should compensate for genetic injustice. One could say that it was wrong to pay the stupid more than the intelligent because society should compensate for the unhappiness which is the usual lot of the intelligent. (No one can do much about the brilliant, they will be miserable anyway.) One could say that it was wrong to pay the man who lived a long and serene life in Upper Slaughter as much as a scientist who wore himself out in the service of knowledge. One could say that it was wrong to pay people who liked their work as much as those who didn't. One could—and did—say anything, and whatever one said it was always with the support of . . . justice.

Thirty years on, the dilemmas remain. Justice, argue some, needs to treat everyone fairly, that is equally, unless there are very good arguments for unequal treatment. That is fair to the underdog but is less than fair to those who, perhaps, "deserve" more, because they contribute more to society. What is clear is that a society perceived to be unjust will earn no loyalty or commitment from its citizens. Such a society is doomed, in the end, to destroy itself.

Capitalism thrives on the first definition of distributive justice—those who achieve most should get most. But it will not long be credible or tolerated if it ignores the other definition, that those who need most should have their needs met. To put it another way, capitalism depends on the fundamental principle of inequality, some may do better than others, but will only be acceptable in the long term in a democracy if most people have an equal chance to aspire to that inequality.

The paradox of justice is the last paradox on my list, but it might be the most important. We cannot afford to ignore it, nor any of the other eight. Since we cannot solve these paradoxes, or make them disappear, we have to learn to live with them. These paradoxes are part of our life, and part of our age.

Finding the Balance

Pathways through Paradox

WORKING WITH THE PARADOXES

● *Working With The Paradoxes*

Paradox confuses us because things don't behave the way we expect them to behave. What worked well last time around is not guaranteed to work as well the next time. Governments seem surprised when each economic recovery soaks up fewer of the unemployed. They have not taken account of the fact that organizations have belatedly realized that it is possible to grow without growing the labor force. They have been used to thinking of organizations as delivery vehicles for social policy, not noticing that, in some countries, they now employ only 55% of the workforce on a full-time basis, which is, in turn, only 38% of all adults of working age. The organizing organization is not the same as the employment organization. Governments need to reframe their view of the world.

Paradox also confuses because it asks us to live with simultaneous opposites. To live with simultaneous opposites is, at first glance, a recipe for indecision at best, schizophrenia at worst. It need not be. My mother-in-law was generous to a fault *and* tight-fisted—she would have called it thrifty. We all knew her ways and understood. We ourselves can, in the same hour, make plans to move house next year *and* decide on the menu for tonight's dinner. Parents are simultaneously tough and strict *and* tender and relaxed with their children. If they do it right, the kids understand. Similarly, organizations are tight *and* loose; concerned only about the longer term in some areas but passionate about detail in others. When we are used to it, and understand it, paradox is no bother.

It is, however, the understanding that is the key. Balancing the opposites, or switching between them, must not be a random or haphazard act. Without a clear rationale for what is happening, the balancing and the switching can be bewildering to those on the receiving end and frustrating for anyone doing the balancing. Without understanding, things do not work out as they should. Living with paradox is like riding a seesaw. If you know how the process works, *and* if the person at the other end also knows, then the ride can be exhilarating. If, however, your opposite number does not understand, or willfully upsets the pattern, you can receive a very uncomfortable and unexpected shock.

As it is with seesaws, so it is with life. If we know how and why things work, we can live with the ups and the downs, knowing opposites are necessary to one another. We can even come to recognize that for the seesaw to work effectively, others must get as good as we get. What follows, in this part of the book, are three general principles for living with simultaneous opposites. You could call them rules for riding seesaws. They are followed, in Part 3, by examples of the principles at work, in our organizations and in society.

3 *The Sigmoid Curve*

The Wicklow Mountains lie just outside Dublin, Ireland. It is an area of wild beauty, a place to which, as an Irishman born near there, I return as often as I can. It is still a bare and lonely spot, with unmarked roads, and I still get lost. Once I stopped and asked the way. "Sure, it's easy," a local replied, "just keep going the way you are, straight ahead, and after a while you'll cross a small bridge with Davy's Bar on the far side. You can't miss it!" "Yes, I've got that," I said. "Straight on to Davy's Bar." "That's right. Well, half a mile before you get there, turn to your right up the hill."

His directions seemed so logical that I thanked him and drove off. By the time I realized that the logic made no sense he had disappeared. As I made my way down to Davy's Bar, wondering which of the roads to the right to take, I reflected that he had just given me a vivid example of paradox, perhaps even the paradox of our times; by the time you know where you ought to go, it's too late to go there, or, more dramatically, if you keep on going the way you are, you will miss the road to the future.

Because, like my Irishman, it is easy to explain things looking backward, we think that we can then predict them forward. It doesn't work, as many economists know to their cost. The world keeps changing. It is one of the paradoxes of success that the things and the ways which got you where you are are seldom those that keep you there. If you think they are, and that you know the way to the future because it is a continuation of where you've come from, you may well end up in Davy's Bar, with nothing left but a chance to drown your sorrows and reminisce about times past.

Although he knew it not, the Irishman had also introduced me to the sigmoid curve, the curve that explains so many of our present discontents and confusions. It is this curve, and what follows from it, that is the first of the pathways through paradox, the first of the three devices for finding a balance between the contradictions.

THE SIGMOID CURVE

The sigmoid curve is the S-shaped curve that has intrigued people since time began. The sigmoid curve sums up the story of life itself. We start slowly, experimentally, and falteringly; we wax and then we wane. It is the story of the British Empire, and of the Soviet Empire, and of all empires always. It is the story of a product's life cycle and of many a corporation's rise and fall. It even describes the course of love and relationships. If that were all, it would be a depressing image. There would be nothing to discuss except to decide where precisely on the curve one is now, and what units of time should go on the scale at the bottom. Those units of time are also getting depressingly small. They used to be decades, perhaps even generations. Now they are years, sometimes months. The accelerating pace of change shrinks every sigmoid curve.

Luckily, there is life beyond the curve. The secret to constant growth is to start a new sigmoid curve before the first one peters out. The right place to start that second curve is at point A where there is the time, as well as the resources and the energy, to get the new curve through its initial explorations and flounderings before the first curve begins to dip downward.

That would seem obvious; were it not for the fact that at point A all the messages coming through to the individual or the institution are that everything is fine, that it would be folly to change when the current recipes are working so well. All that we know of change, be it personal or organizational, tells us that the real energy for change comes only when you are looking disaster in the face, at point B on the first curve.

At this point, however, it is going to require a mighty effort to drag oneself up to where, by now, one should be on the second curve. To make it worse, the current leaders are discredited because they are perceived to have led the organization down the hill. Furthermore, resources are depleted and energies are low. For an individual, an event like being laid off typically takes place at point B. At that point, it is hard to mobilize the resources or to re-store the credibility which one had at the peak. There-fore, we should not be surprised that people get de-pressed at this point or that institutions invariably start the change process, if they leave it until point B, by bring-ing in new people at the top, because only people new to the situation will have the credibility and the vision to lift the place back onto the second curve.

Wise are they who start the second curve at point A because that is the pathway through paradox, the way to build a new future while maintaining the present. Even then the problems do not end. The second curve, be it a new product, a new way of operating, a new strategy, or a new culture, is going to be noticeably different from the old. It has to be. The people also have to be different. Those who lead the second curve are often not the people who led the first curve. For one thing, the responsi-bility of those original leaders is to keep that first curve going long enough to support the early stages of the sec-ond curve. For another, they will find it temperamentally difficult to abandon the first curve while it is doing so well, even if they recognize, intellectually, that a new curve is needed. For a time, therefore, new ideas and new people have to co-exist with the old until the second curve is es-tablished and the first begins to wane.

The shaded area is, therefore, a time of great confu-sion. Two, or more, groups of people and two sets of ideas are competing for the future. No matter how wise and benevolent they may be, the leaders of the first curve must worry about their own futures when their curve be-gins to die. Only if they can move onto the second curve will they have a continuing life in the organization. If they cannot join that second curve they should leave, but it requires great foresight, and even greater magnanimity, to foster others and plan one's own departure. Those who can do it, however, will ensure the renewal and the continued growth of their organization.

I cannot pretend that is easy even with that foresight. I have watched the chairman of a great company speak to his assembled barons. "I have two messages for you today," he said. "First, I want to remind you that we are a very successful business, perhaps more successful today than we have ever been. Secondly, I must tell you that if we want to continue to be successful we shall have to change, fundamentally, the way we are working now." He went on to explain why the different futures he foresaw would require different responses, but no one was listening. The first message had drowned out the second. If they were so successful, they felt, it would be folly to change. He was right. He was standing at point A and looking over the hill, but he could not get his changes implemented. Three years later, by now at point B, the company knew it had to change, but the first person it turned on, and removed, was the chairman. He was no longer credible, nor had his conviction that he was right endeared him to his colleagues. He had failed as a leader, not because he was wrong in sensing the need for a second curve but because he had not managed to get them to share his understanding. Those who can do that at point A and not at point B are the leaders we all need.

What is true of organizations is true of individuals and their relationships. A good life is probably a succession of second curves, started before the first curve fades. Lives and priorities change as one grows up and older. Every relationship will sometime need its second curve. Too often, couples cling to their old habits and contracts for too long. By the time they realize the need for that second curve they are already at point B. It is too late to do it together. They find other partners. On the other hand, I sometimes like to say, teasingly, that I am on my second marriage—but with the same partner, which makes it less expensive. Because we managed, in time, to find that very different second curve—together. I would not deny, however, that the shaded portion beneath the peak was a difficult time as we struggled to keep what was best in our past while we experimented with the new.

I sense that many institutions, many individuals, and even whole societies, are in that shaded period right now. It is a time of great confusion, uncertainty, and fear. People do not understand why things that have worked so well up to now no longer do the trick. That first curve is peaking everywhere. Some people, understandably, want to prolong the old ways indefinitely. Others actively search for the new.

Capitalism, newly triumphant, probably has to re-invent itself. Things which we took for granted, like nation-states and large organizations, seem to be impediments to progress, not its helpers. When both the British monarchy and the judiciary are seen wanting, few institutions in the country can be sure that they are still on the upward curve. We ask our politicians for a lead, by which we mean a sight of the second curve, but, all the same, we want them to do nothing to disturb the first. In our personal lives we sense there is often another hill to climb now that life is longer and, in many ways, larger, but we have no sense of where to find that hill. So many of us are living in that hazed area, worrying that the first curve will turn down before we find the second.

That second curve is the road up the hill to the

right. Today we stand at the crossroads, asking the way to the future. It is a place of paradox, a confusion of simultaneous opposites, of unexpected consequences, of altered meanings, and oxymorons. Words like "hierarchy," "loyalty," and "duty" no longer carry the weight they once did. Other words like "freedom," "choice," and "rights" turn out to be more complicated than they seemed. What was once obvious, like the necessity of economic growth, is now hedged with qualifications. We thought we knew how to run organizations, but the organizations of today bear no resemblance to the ones we knew, and so we have to find the second curve of management before it is too late. Meanwhile, we have to keep the first curve going. In that way we can manage to live with paradox because we understand what is happening.

THE DISCIPLINE OF THE
SECOND CURVE

The concept of the sigmoid curve has, I find, helped many people and many institutions understand their current confusions. The question they always ask, however, is: How do we know where we are on the first curve? One way of answering is to ask them to make their own private and personal assessment of their position, or that of their organization: draw the first curve as they see it, and to mark an X on it to show where they are now. Almost invariably, when they reveal their perceptions of the curve, there is a consensus that they are further along the curve than any of them would previously have admitted. They are nearer to point B than to point A.

Like the story of the road to Davy's Bar, you will only know for sure where you are on the curve when you look back. It is easier, too, to see where others are on their curves than to see yourself. Therefore, we must proceed by guess and assumption. There is no science for this sort of thing. The discipline of the second curve requires that you always assume that you are near the peak of the first curve, at point A, and should therefore be starting to prepare for the second. Organizations should assume that their present strategies will need to be replaced within two or three years and that their product life cycles are shorter than they were. Richard Foster of McKinsey studied 208 companies over 18 years to discover those that were consistently successful. There were only three that lasted the course for the whole 18 years. Fifty-three percent could not maintain their record for more than two years. Individuals should also work on the assumption that a new direction will be needed in two or three years.

It may well be that the assumption turns out to be wrong, that the present trends can be prolonged much longer, and that the first curve was really only in its infancy. Nothing has been lost. Only the exploratory phase of the second curve has been done. No major commitments will have been undertaken until the second curve overtakes the first, which will never happen as long as the first curve is still on the rise. Keeping the two curves going will become a habit.

The discipline of devising that second curve will, however, have had its effect. It will have forced one to challenge the assumptions underlying the first curve and to devise some possible alternatives. The discipline of the second curve keeps one sceptical, curious, and inventive—attitudes essential in a time of change, and the best way of coping with the contradictions that accompany such a time.

The discipline of the second curve follows the traditional four-stage cycle of discovery. Questions start it off. The questions give rise to ideas, possibilities, hypotheses. The best of these must then be tested out, tentatively and experimentally. Finally, the results of the experiments are reviewed. The first two stages cost nothing except the time for imagination. They can be very stimulating, particularly if they start from the greenfield hypothesis: "If we did not exist, would we re-invent ourselves and, if so, what would we look like?" Or, in a more personal example of second-curve thinking: "If we did not live here, or do what we are doing, what would we be doing, where and how would we be living if we had the chance to start again?" The discipline of the second curve means that you do not re-invent the same life because that would merely perpetuate the first curve. The second curve is always different, although it builds on and grows out of the first.

In *The Paradox of Success*, his book on the personal renewal of leaders, John O'Neil uses the model of the second curve to describe how leaders do, or do not, move on in life. He points out that one essential is to let go of your past. If one is too emotionally attached to what has gone before, it is difficult to be different in any way. He quotes Odysseus as an example of a young warrior chief who was so committed to roaming and raiding, at which he once excelled, that he spent 20 years returning from the Trojan War to his kingdom of Ithaca, reluctant to assume the responsibilities of governing. By the time he got home, he was a failed commander, in rags, and his kingdom was a mess. This is the story of the man who did not want to grow up.

If success comes early, it can be particularly hard to turn one's back on it when one's star begins to wane. It was sad to watch Björn Borg return to the tennis courts in an attempt to recapture past glories, long after his talents had faded. It is often easier to move on from disasters than from successes. I have always been impressed by people like Leonard Cheshire, the distinguished and heroic British fighter pilot who, after World War II was over, created a network of homes for the elderly and disabled. I am impressed by the family business in France that, at just the right time, turned its back on the textile industry in which it had made its name and launched a chain of supermarkets. "Where did you find the courage to do something so completely different?," I asked the head of the family. "It would have required more courage to do nothing," she replied. "We had the responsibility to provide a future for the family, and the past, distinguished though it was, could not have been that future."

CURVILINEAR LOGIC

Moving on requires a belief in what Schumacher used to call curvilinear logic, the conviction that the world and everything in it really is a sigmoid curve, that everything has its ups and then its downs, and that nothing lasts forever or was there forever. Just-in-time manufacturing was developed in Japan, and copied everywhere. The idea of a constant stream of materials delivered to your factory door as and when you needed them was blindingly obvious when you thought about it. Cut out the warehouse and all those storage costs. Let the suppliers carry the inventory costs, or rather, eliminate them completely, provided that you can always guarantee that the trucks with the bits will arrive just-in-time. Unfortunately the idea got too popular—delivery vehicles now jam all the freeways around Tokyo, meaning that just-in-time often gives way to just-too-late. The costs of the traffic jams are beginning to outweigh the costs of the original warehouses, to say nothing of the environmental damage caused by idling exhausts. You can have too much of a good thing.

Curvilinear logic is not intuitively obvious if you are still ascending the first curve. Business history is littered with the stories of founding fathers who thought that their way was the only way. The French textile business mentioned above is a notable rarity among family businesses. The paradox of success, that what got you where you are won't keep you where you are, is a hard lesson to learn. Curvilinear logic means starting life over again, something that gets harder as one gets older. Therefore, it is often better, in organizations, to entrust the curvilinear thinking to the next generation. It can see more clearly where the first curve is heading and what the next curve might look like. It is the job of the elders to give that cohort permission to be different, and then, when the next curve is established, to get out of the way. For that to happen, there has to be a new curve for them, outside.

"My father brought me back from America to run the business here in Treviso," grumbled the daughter. "But he still comes into the office every day, even Sundays. He wants me to run the business as if I was him, and I'm not. And the business has to change if he would only let it. It's very frustrating." Her story is not unusual. The father had nothing else he wanted to do. The business had been his life, and now he had no other. "Wet leaves we call them in Japan," said the Japanese lady, describing the reaction of Japan's women to their retired executive husbands. "You know how it is with wet leaves, they just stick around!" For curvilinear logic to work in an organization there has to be a life beyond the organization for the leaders of the first curve.

On the face of it, the Coca-Cola Company is the great exception to the concept of the second curve. For 104 years it has sold the same product in the same packaging with much the same advertising. The only time it changed the formula it was forced by its customers to reverse the decision. Its secret, however, may lie in the motto that is inscribed in the central offices and in the minds of all its officers: "The world belongs to the discontented." It was the favorite saying of their early and long-time chairman, Robert Woodruff. He was warning against complacency and advocating a perpetual curiosity—the itch of the second curve. Coca-Cola's Japanese company, I was told, test-markets a new soft drink variety or other product every month. Even if most of them fail most of the time, it keeps the questing spirit alive. When and if Coca-Cola's 104-year curve turns down, it hopes that it will be prepared.

The Japanese, of course, have their own word for it—*kaizen,* or continuous improvement. The assumption behind kaizen is the assumption behind this book: there is no perfect answer in a changing world. We must be forever searching. Anita Roddick, of The Body Shop, puts it more succinctly: "What is so wonderful about The Body Shop is that we still don't know the rules." As long as it thinks that way, so long will it thrive. Complacency is the enemy of curiosity.

The Royal Dutch Shell Group has yet another approach. They call it scenario planning. It has been well explained by Peter Schwartz, one of the members of the planning group, in his book *The Art of the Long View.* A group of executives, aided by some outsiders, spends a year or more drawing up alternative scenarios for the oil business and the countries and cultures in which it operates. These are not plans but possibilities, deliberately set at opposite ends of a spectrum. The planning group uses these scenarios educationally, exposing their managers around the world to the alternatives and asking them to consider how they would respond if either happened. Shell planners want no surprises, and were not surprised by the oil crisis of the early 1970s nor by the collapse of the Soviet Empire. Their second-curve thinking was ready. It was not so, says Schwartz, in the case of the American military. It made every sort of contingency plan for the Cold War but never asked the scenario question "What if we won?" When they did win, they knew not what to do with the victory.

Peter Senge, in his classic book on the learning organization, reminds us that our mental models, or private scenarios, are crucial to the learning process. We all carry mental maps around with us—that hierarchy is natural, for instance, that women can't manage, or that men don't care; that careers last until we are 65 or that every next job has to be a promotion. We need to check and see if these assumptions are still valid because they lock us into our existing curve. They inhibit second-curve thinking. My first book on organizations was written 20 years ago. Quite unconsciously, I used the male pronoun exclusively throughout the book. It became a standard text, used by those training to work in schools, hospitals, and the social services as well as business. My book caused a great deal of offense to the many women who had to study it because it seemed that I, the supposed authority, thought there was no place for them in management. My mental map of 20 years ago only mirrored what many men felt then, and some still do. That map locked them into their first curve; it made it difficult for them to envisage another kind of world and another way of doing things. It was not only offensive, it was harmful.

Many of the ideas in this book stem from second-curve thinking—the discipline that says that the past might not be the best guide to the future, that there can be another way, and that some "myths of the future," as Schwartz calls them, will help. We must, however, be wary that we do not abandon the first curve too early. The second curve needs the resources and the time that only the first curve can provide. "Dreams give wings to fools," my young daughter used to tell me when she heard me fantasizing about other lives we might live. She was expressing her instinct that the future needs to be rooted in the past if it is to be real. The secret of balance in a time of paradox is to allow the past and the future to co-exist in the present.

FERTILIZING
THE SECOND CURVE

Second-curve thinking will come most naturally from the second generation, those who will inherit the future. They will, however, need both permission and encouragement. They must realize that what they might privately think of as revolution, or even sedition, because it challenges the way things are now, is possibly the way ahead, that new ideas can co-exist with old.

One organization openly entrusted its second-curve thinking to a group of executives in their early thirties. It happened, however, almost by accident. They wanted to celebrate the twenty-fifth anniversary of their organization. Their first thought was to commission a history of those first 25 years. That seemed, on reflection, to be self-indulgent and uninteresting. They decided instead to commission an outside look at the next 25 years for their industry. They were then persuaded that the most fruitful way to do that would be to entrust that look to the brightest and best of their own people, people who might be leading their organization when those years arrived. The look at the future should, therefore, include some thoughts and recommendations on how the organization should adapt to the changes they might foresee for their industry and the world around them. They were giving these young people the responsibility for their own inheritance.

I was asked to act as mentor to the study. I agreed, provided that the board of the organization agreed to publish the nonconfidential part of the exercise as a booklet without censoring it in any way. The board agreed, but went further. It offered to invite all the firm's customers to a reception to celebrate the anniversary, to listen to a presentation of the findings of the group, and to receive a free copy of the uncensored booklet. The effect of this advance commitment was impressive. The group saw that this was not some ingenious educational exercise but a genuine attempt to build some new thinking into the existing fabric of the organization. It was being publicly trusted by its seniors to develop some new thinking. The seniors were not only impressed by the results of the study, they took them to heart. Their advance commitment had ensured that they would not feel it necessary to defend the status quo, the first curve, and squash the beginnings of the second.

It is important that the seniors give permission and encouragement. It is also important that the next generation accept responsibility for second-curve thinking. Preoccupied with the immediacy of their own careers, young people are tempted to think that second-curve thinking can be left until later, that the present is their priority, the future the priority of those in charge. In actual fact, it should be the other way round.

I helped, once, to organize what came to be called the Windsor Meetings. They took place at St. George's House, a small study center in the middle of Windsor Castle, often used for weekend gatherings of influential individuals to discuss, privately and informally, social and ethical issues. There were, inevitably, discussions about the present, because the people who came were in charge of the present. We decided, with the help and support of some businesses, to bring together representatives of the next generation of influential people from all sectors of society who were identified as likely future leaders in their spheres.

Thus it was that a young colonel, tapped as a future general, found himself in the company of an up-and-coming trade union official, a talented young headmistress, a banker, some civil servants, three of the younger and more thoughtful politicians from the different parties, a campaigner for human rights, the new editor of a quality newspaper, a television newscaster, a doctor and a lawyer, five business executives—all successful people in their thirties, but preoccupied with their own careers, too busy, at this stage, to look outside or to know anyone not involved in their line of work. They were all at the lower end of their personal first curves, and rising fast. Invited to Windsor Castle, as guests, for the inside of a week, they were asked to debate and discuss the shape of the society that they would inherit.

Few of them had thought about such broad issues. None of them had been exposed to such a wide range of other interests. Their discussions were always stimulating and their reports insightful, but the ultimate benefit was the realization that they had a responsibility to help shape the future. It was a consciously elitist exercise because if those soon to be in power are not conscious of their responsibility to shape a second curve, who is? Many of those groups still meet because, in spite of their very different preoccupations, they found that they also shared a concern for the future of their society, that it would be civilized as well as rich, humane as well as adventurous. There is strength in companionship when it comes to shaping the second curve. We have to hope that, when and if they reach positions of eminence, they will not forget their commitment to that second curve.

Both of these examples used insiders. Some organizations prefer outsiders, believing they may have a more objective view and a clearer perspective. Consultants thrive on contracts for what are, effectively, second-curve thinking. The thinking, however, is only part of it. There needs to be the commitment to carry it through, to endure the early dip before the curve climbs upward, to live with the first curve while the second one develops. These things cannot be done by outsiders. To manage paradox, you need to live with it as well as analyze it.

4 *The Doughnut Principle*

The doughnut in question is an American doughnut, the kind with a hole in the middle, rather than the British version, which has jam instead of a hole. The doughnut principle, however, requires an inside-out doughnut, one with the hole on the outside and the dough in the middle. Therefore, it can only be a conceptual dough-nut, one for thinking with, not eating.

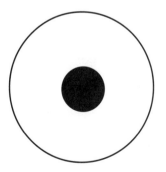

A doughnut may seem to be an unlikely pathway through paradox, but the concept of balancing a core and a bounded space is crucial to a proper understanding of most of life, as I hope to show. It is a way to find the balance between what we have to do and what we could do or could be.

We might look, for instance, at our job, our paid job or our unpaid role in life, as parent, wife, husband or carer, student, or friend. The heart of the doughnut, the core, contains all the things which must be done in that job or role if you are to succeed. In a formal job, these things are listed as your duties. Even when they are not listed, these duties are often well understood. The core, however, is not the whole of the doughnut. If it were, life would be all chore as well as core. There is, thankfully, the space beyond. This space is our opportunity to make a difference, to go beyond the bounds of duty, to live up to our full potential. That remains our ultimate responsibility in life, a responsibility always larger than duty, just as the doughnut is larger than its core.

The doughnut image is a conceptual way of relating duty to a fuller responsibility in every institution or group in society. Doughnuts stimulate our thinking about the proper equation between commitments and flexibility, in the structures of our work as well as in our personal life. We can draw a doughnut to represent a relationship, or an organization, or a work group, just as we can use it to reveal the balance in our own life between work and family or between necessity and choice. It is a visual tool for balancing what often seem to be contradictions.

Much of life now looks like that doughnut. Organizations as well as individuals have come to realize that they have an essential core, a core of necessary jobs and necessary people, a core which is surrounded by an open flexible space, which they fill with flexible workers and flexible supply contracts. The strategic issue for organizations, nowadays, is to decide what activities and which people to put in which space. It is not always obvious. Looked at in another way, businesses have core obligations to their shareholders, but their responsibilities go much further. Finding the right balance between duty and a wider responsibility is a dilemma at the heart of capitalism.

Schools, in most countries, have a required core curriculum, with discretionary space around it. The argument, again, is about balance. What, and how much, should go in which space? Too much core leaves no room for individual student differences or for local school initiatives. Too much space means there is too much variety in the standards of delivery.

We can apply the doughnut principle to processes as well as to structures. Reward systems tend to lay down the minimum remuneration with space for options, bonuses, and performance money. Our implied contracts within our personal relationships contain a core of obligations, with space for individual differences around the core. In your marriage, said Khalil Gibran in *The Prophet,* which is read at countless weddings and then too often forgotten, you should stand together, but "let there be space in your togetherness." What every couple needs to define, however, is what should go into that space and what the boundaries are to be. A marriage without boundaries is, I suspect, an unreal doughnut and doomed to fail. Every couple could, with advantage, draw their own doughnut.

The doughnut principle starts early. I remember my own schooldays. I had passed the big examination but my disappointed teacher, obviously quite distressed by my results, confronted me. "What's wrong?" I said. "I passed, didn't I? Isn't that enough?" "Enough is never enough," he replied, "until you have exhausted your potential. To pass was easy. You could have done better, much better." Enough is never enough. I recall John Donne's lines, "When you have done, you have not done, for there is more." To pass was the essential core. To fill the doughnut I had to do more. Life, my teacher was trying to tell me, should not be a half-filled doughnut. I have spent most of the rest of my life wondering how I ought to fill it.

That principle now applies to much of our work. That ugly word "empowerment" could better be interpreted as the doughnut principle at work. In the past, jobs used to be all core, certainly at the lower levels, because too much discretion meant too much unpredictability. One of my early jobs had the fine-sounding title of Regional Co-ordination Marketing (Oil) Mediterranean Region. My friends were impressed, but they did not know the reality. The reality was a three-page job description outlining my duties, but the hard truth was contained in the final paragraph: "Authority to initiate expenditure up to a maximum of £10." My doughnut was all core and no space. That way the organization got no surprises, or so it hoped. All was predictable, planned, and controlled. It was also dull and frustrating, with no space for self-expression, no space to make a difference, no empowerment. My memoranda came from my role—MK/32—not from me. I was merely a "temporary role occupant" and I felt like an empty raincoat.

There are some people, on the other hand, whose jobs are nearly all space with little core and no boundary. Ministers of religion have a visible core to their work—

the church services, visits to the sick, committees, and finances—but there is no limit to their responsibilities for the souls of their congregation or for their evangelizing work. Some of the most stressed people I have known have been people with jobs like these, because there is no end, no way in which you can look back and say, "It was a great year" because it could always have been greater. Empowerment, in a sense, has gone too far. Without a boundary it is easy to be oppressed by guilt, for enough is never enough. Entrepreneurs revel in the space for discretion, but the successful ones are careful to give themselves targets and limits. Even then, the record of early entrepreneurship is one of long days and no holidays, of unremitting effort to fill the space beyond the core. A sensible job is a balanced doughnut.

TYPE 2
ACCOUNTABILITY

More space, in fact, is not always welcomed, even in a conventional job. More space means more choice but also, paradoxically, more room for error, or, more precisely, another type of error. In statistics, as I recall, there are two types of error. There is type 1 error which, in simple terms, means getting it wrong, and type 2 error which, in effect, means not getting it right, or as right as it could have been. There is an important difference. Type 2 error means that the full possibilities of the situation have not been exploited or developed; enough was not enough. In the old, tightly planned world where everything was contained in the inner circle you only had to look out for type 1 errors. As long as you avoided those you could call yourself successful.

Management was easier, too, since its priority was to check for type 1 errors. Avoid those and the system was designed to deliver. For many people, life was keeping one's nose clean, compiling, as the years went by, a fault-free *curriculum vitae*, lived by the book, with retirement as the promised rest and reward. "He walked in many corridors of power," someone said of a politician, "and left no footprint in any of them." It was a life free of type 1 errors.

It was also a life devoid of type 2 errors. These are the errors of omission not commission, the things one did not do which one could have, the failure to fill the space between the circles. The old prayer book of the Anglican Church put it nicely, I realized as I mumbled my way through the familiar words one day: "We have left undone those things which we ought to have done [type 2] and done those things which we ought not to have done [type 1]." I used to think that what was meant by the first bit were those chores I had neglected, the difficult meetings I had put off, the letters I had not written, but those, I realized, are all type 1 errors. The important sins of omission are the things I did not do which could have made a difference. Enough is not enough.

We hanker after the freedom of more space in our lives and our work; leaner, flatter organizations provide that space, but now it is up to us to fill the space. We used to be held accountable only for type 1 errors; now we have a new accountability, for the things we could have done but didn't. The two accountabilities are a new fact of life. With space goes responsibility. Only when that is generally accepted will we be able to have a truly free society, one in which the freedom to be what you want to be is accompanied by the responsibility to do no harm to others (type 1) and to use the freedom to some purpose (type 2).

One day, too, our public bodies will recognize that it is not enough to make no mistakes, type 1 accountability; it is also important to have done the work as well as it could have been done, to have been better than expected. Public accountability needs to be redefined to include the recognition of type 2 responsibilities.

PERSONAL
DOUGHNUTS

Some people make their work the whole of their life. That necessary core of the job fills the whole doughnut, leaving little or no space for anything else. Are they right or wise? There is an argument that capitalist businesses do not exist as, theoretically at least, communist structures did, to liberate and develop people's humanity and allow them to become moral, fulfilled human beings. Existential development, says Britain's Elizabeth Vallance, is not the primary aim of business but of churches or educational or artistic institutions. Businesses will look to the self-development of their people only to enhance their ability to make profits. If she is right, those who seek their fulfillment in demanding business jobs are likely to be disappointed. It would probably be no better if they worked full-time for her churches or educational or artistic establishments. In the organizations of a capitalist society, the individual is, strictly speaking, the instrument not the purpose.

In contrast, there is the view that all work should be a calling or vocation; that the wealth creation of business is as worth doing and as valuable as the health creation of a hospital. We can and should, that argument goes, get fulfillment out of our work. There is no single answer. The doughnut principle suggests that if you cannot get existential development from your current job, you should either change jobs or make sure that the empty spaces in your personal doughnut are filled somewhere else. One job does not have to fill all needs.

I used to think that it should. I looked for a job that would provide me with interesting and exciting work, work, too, that I would be proud of doing. I also wanted enough money and the chance to make more of it if I needed to, good companions and a pleasing location with the chance of travel. Needless to say, I never found the perfect job. There was, however, a doughnut solution. If I adopted a "portfolio" approach to life, meaning that I saw my life as a collection of different groups and activities, I could get different things from different bits, done for different people. A part of that portfolio would be "core," providing the essential wherewithal for life, but it would be balanced by work done purely for interest or for a cause, or because it would stretch me personally, or simply because it was fascinating or fun.

It was easier, I found, to make money, if that was all that you were concerned with, than if you tried to combine money making with the other attributes. Similarly, it

was easier to find work that was involving and worthwhile if you weren't too concerned about the pay. It
meant, however, turning down the offer of one of those
70-hour-a-week jobs which would have left no time for
anything else, and putting together a package of different
kinds of work, a work portfolio. Now my life is doughnut
shaped. I can even specify the number of days I am prepared to allocate to core activities and those left over for
personal space. As I get older, the core begins to shrink,
leaving me with the interesting but difficult problem of
how best to fill the space beyond the core, to live up to
my responsibility for my life.

Increasingly it should be possible to arrange a portfolio of different sorts of work within the same organization,
by joining a number of their doughnuts. Wise organizations recognize the advantages of these internal portfolios. Different tasks and different groups bring out different
talents in the individual, they confront him or her with
different experiences. Some businesses now actively encourage their staff to take on voluntary activities in the
community, allowing them time off from work if necessary.
Other organizations are happy to see their executives
teaching at a local college, serving on a school board, or
standing for political office. It is, they say, an excellent form
of development. It is also a way of building a work portfolio with the company's blessing.

There are fewer, smaller cores in the job doughnuts
these days, in all spheres and levels of work. If we wait
around for someone to tell us what to do, we shall wait a
long time. If we look for a sure way through life, one
guaranteed to get us through to the end, we shall be disappointed. We have to fill our own spaces.

Societies that overemphasize the core can be too regimented. A place for everyone and everyone in their place was Plato's version of a just society, but it meant that everyone's role in life was predetermined, all core and very little space for individuality. It was an idea that still lingered on in Britain when I first came to live and work there, even though the core was more socially determined than official. There were strong norms on dress and behavior. "Wear brown on Sundays," I was told, "and never telephone anyone after 10 o'clock at night." I envy the freedom of my children and their friends who respect neither of those conventions nor many others, but they have the burden of too much space. There are too many choices of careers and too many varieties of life-styles. It is no longer mandatory to be married in order to be a parent, let alone to share a home. It is hard for them to see what the core of life can be apart from earning the bare necessities, and even those will, if need be, come from the state.

They have the freedom to design their own doughnuts. They would be wise to give themselves both core and boundaries, a baseline for the kind of life they want to live and areas they will not touch, things they will not do, rules of conduct to which they will adhere. A society that emphasizes rights but neglects obligations can leave too much space for its citizens. The problem for the unemployed is not so much that they are hungry but that they have no core to their lives. Empty doughnuts are not easy to live with, any more than doughnuts which are all core.

Work, moreover, is no longer organized as it used to be. Organizations are not now drawn as pyramids of boxes. British Steel is said to have had an organization chart which, when unfolded, stretched across a room. Those charts now have circles and amoeba-like blobs where boxes used to be. It isn't even clear where the organization begins and ends, with customers, suppliers, and allied organizations linked into a "network organization." Work no longer means, for everyone, having a "job" with an employer. As organizations disperse and contract themselves, more and more of us will be working for ourselves, often by ourselves.

The new shape of work will center around small organizations, most of them in the service sector, with a small core of key people and a collection of stringers or portfolio workers in the space around the core. David Birch, an economist with the research organization Cognetics, studied the job market in the United States from 1987 to 1991. He found that the big firms laid off a net 2.4 million workers in that period, while firms with fewer than 20 employees added 4.4 million new jobs, with slightly larger firms adding another 1.4 million. Nor were all these jobs, this time around, hamburger jobs. Software, telecommunications, environmental engineering, health products and services, and specialized education are increasingly the province of the tiny partnership. They are all well suited to the portfolio worker, who costs much less if the firm does not have to house him or her. Their work, and that of their larger brothers, increasingly fits the doughnut pattern.

We can see the doughnut pattern most obviously when we look at the new-style organizations. The $1/2 \times 2 \times 3$ formula, which all organizations have to work toward in this competitive age, means that these days every organization has its smaller core and its surrounding partnerships. Some of these partners are traditional suppliers, some are independent professionals, some are the part-time peripheral workers, and some are the allied businesses, partners in joint ventures of one sort or another.

Balancing the core and the surrounding space is never easy. The British government, in an attempt to reduce costs, is "market-testing" many of its traditional core activities. Functions which have traditionally been done by the core civil service are now required to be tested for cost and performance against outside bids. If they compare unfavorably, the activity moves into the space of the doughnut. The collection of Britain's National Insurance contributions, a form of wages tax worth nearly £40 billion a year, is one activity proposed for such market testing. There are, however, some reasonable concerns that it would be too risky to contract out such a vital source of national revenue. Some people feel it should be designated a core activity, impervious to market testing. The Home Office is contemplating putting activities as diverse as the Criminal Injuries Compensation Board, the Customs control at ports and airports, and even the Research and Planning Unit out for bid. The BBC's contentious policy of "producer choice," under which all decisions have to be market-tested, means that the doughnut balance of the corporation is being decided piecemeal, by individual producers, on a short-term cost basis. Many fear that this process is not guaranteed as the best way to arrive at a long-term strategic balance, at the optimum doughnut for the BBC.

Businesses routinely put their materials suppliers in the space of their corporate doughnuts. The vertically integrated organization, one that wanted to own and run the whole of its doughnut, is a thing of the past. Some, however, also contract out crucial service functions. Eastman Kodak sees the sense in contracting out its entire information system. Others turn over their strategy formulation to consultants. There is no limit to what you can, if you want to, put in the space of the doughnut. It is the balance that is crucial. The British Civil Service is worried about the effects on morale if too many of the key elements of its work are privatized. Short-term savings may result in long-term damage if a demoralized service fails to recruit new talent. There is no neat general answer. It is always a question of finding the appropriate balance.

Others worry that the new partners may effectively become part of the core if they are bonded too tightly. Flexibility, which was the point of the doughnut structure, disappears if the supplier becomes dependent on one customer for most of its business, or the firm on one supplier. Contracts should be flexible, experience suggests, and not more than 30% of capacity or requirements should be tied to any one outfit.

Ricardo Semler, president of Semco in Brazil, deliberately designs his whole company as a doughnut, or what he would call a double circle, with a group of counsellors in the middle and all the other workers, the partners and associates, as he terms them, in the outer space. They are then held together in smaller doughnuts, or circles, by coordinators. Managing doughnuts is the new organizational challenge. It is a challenge because one is managing the doughnut, and its different spaces, rather than the person. Managing other people's spaces is not easy. It is no longer the manager and the managed, but the designer of the doughnut and the occupant—a different relationship, one built more on trust and mutual respect than on control.

Organizations everywhere are being "re-invented" or "re-engineered." They are breaking down, or rather, blowing up their functions and their old ways of working and are re-grouping people, equipment, and systems around a particular task. They are creating work doughnuts, groups with complete responsibility for discharging the task, with specified rules and duties—the core—and a lot of discretionary space to do it in the way that they think best. The results can be startling. The most famous is Ford's accounts payable department which thought it had done well when it reduced staff by 20%, to 400, until they found that Mazda did the job with only 5 people! Ford thought again and got their numbers down to 100, the $1/2 \times 2 \times 3$ formula beaten twice over. The term "Business Re-Engineering" has been patented by a consulting firm, but the concept at its heart is as old as the doughnut. Ian Gibson, chief executive of Nissan Motor Manufacturing in Britain, told the graduating class of the London Business School that his first discipline was physics:

> I tend to think of things in a scientist's terms—in this case in terms of the difference between crystalline and amorphous structures. As an example, the most easy way to recognize a crystalline structure is in a dia-

mond, and perhaps the most common, if unglamorous, amorphous material is mud. The typical western organization is crystalline; clearly defined, facets that have their own shape, with obvious joints between them. The features of our organizations are comparable— clear definitions of role and responsibilities; well-defined boundaries within different parts of the organization; each part of the organization in a known and fixed relationship to the others.

In contrast, Japanese organizations are more like mud. They are far more blurred, separation between responsibilities and functions is ill-defined and in a constant state of flux. Reverting to the analogy, a diamond is clear, tough and precise. Mud is vague, it changes shape and form. It has, however, one over-riding benefit—it is easily shaped and changed and is flexible and responsive to external forces and circumstances. As organizations, we must become increasingly able to change quickly and easily. This means building on and around people's abilities rather than limiting them for the convenience of easily recognized roles.

The doughnut organization is even laid out, physically, as a doughnut. The center no longer dominates from a headquarters tower block. It is smaller and more club-like, with outlying or satellite offices around the country. Frank Becker, who is leading an American project called Workscape 21 at Cornell University, believes that more and more workers will split time between a central office, a computer-equipped home office, and a satellite office in a suburban business park. The central office itself will be doughnut-shaped, built around "common rooms," which will increasingly resemble hotel lobbies or the rooms of a clubhouse.

I was meeting with the senior executive group of one of the country's leading manufacturers of office furniture. The subject for discussion was the executive suite of the future—what sort of furniture would it require. We decided to start by quizzing Anita, the human resources director, on how she spent a typical working week, in order to get some feel of how she uses her office. In the past month, it turned out, Anita had worked out of hotel rooms, airplanes, and airport lounges, on the premises of the subsidiary businesses, and at home in the evenings and early mornings. She had spent two Friday afternoons in her office, collecting the nonurgent mail and checking schedules with her secretary. The only classy furniture she really needed was a bag to hold her bits and pieces of electronic equipment. For her, the office was a club, which she checked into occasionally.

DOUGHNUT THINKING

This has, for me, been the year of funerals. I have listened to many a eulogy on the life of old friends or relatives. Those eulogies always relate the facts and the distinctions of the life now ended, but they go on to the important and most interesting bit—a description of the person as she was to those who knew and loved her. By the time we die, I realized again and again, our doughnuts have to be complete. The real "us" is, ironically, not in the core but in the whole, if we think of the core as the necessities of life, that curriculum vitae which most of us so assiduously compile in the earlier part of our lives. It is up to us, and only us, to fill the space before we die.

I seldom know, in any detail, what it is that my friends really do in their work because when we meet we talk of other things. Ironically, I think, I like them better when they are not succeeding, and they me likewise because then there is more space and time for friends and fun. To put it crudely, they, and I, are less boring when less successful. There is more space in our doughnuts. The answer is not to be a total failure, but to get the balance right, to prepare oneself for that ultimate eulogy to your grieving friends.

We overdo the core. In our personal lives we often exaggerate the necessities. Few need as much as they think that they do, or as much security as they hanker after. Organizations build bigger cores than they need, and impose bigger cores on their internal doughnuts than are necessary. Schools, everywhere, impose timetables on their students, filling their hours with things they are required to do. In a world which seems filled with rules and duties, responsibility goes unregarded. Even the rules and duties become devalued, as we instinctively reject the idea that so much of us can be prescribed. No one wants an empty doughnut, one with no obligations and no commitments, but one with too large a core breeds a sense of impotence.

We find it a paradox that people clamor for rights but ignore their responsibilities, that people want democracy but expect others to sort out all its problems for them, that people complain when others take initiative but take no initiative themselves. We find it odd that there is so little time to enjoy the fruits of our labors, but later find that we don't know how to enjoy the fruits when we do have time. We are unused to all that space in our lives. We have been so burdened with duties that we have never learned the delights of responsibility, of making a difference to someone or something.

By overemphasizing the duties and the rules of the core, organizations unintentionally breed distrust. A £10 discretionary authority hardly indicates confidence in one's judgment or integrity. Obsessed by the need to control, firms create self-fulfilling prophecies when their people learn that the only way to be independent is to break the rules. My children learned to smoke because the schools they went to made nonsmoking a rule, the implicit message being: "We don't believe that you will heed the warnings about the dangers of nicotine, so we will make it a core obligation." Such a deliberate denial of responsibility made it legitimate, in the eyes of the students, to ignore the rule. Smoking became a symbol of free choice, of personal space in their doughnut. If we do not allow people space, we cannot always expect responsible behavior. There are risks, of course. Not everyone can handle the same amounts of space and responsibility. Doughnuts have to be adjusted to the capacity of the individual or the group. As parents we allow more space as children grow, but always within boundaries. The risks of not doing it, the type 2 error of restricting space, are, however, much more serious. Too much space can cause an error or an accident. Too little can impoverish a life.

5 *The Chinese Contract*

I remember my first exposure to the Chinese contract. I
was the manager in South Malaysia for an oil company,
responsible for, among other things, negotiating agency
agreements with our Chinese dealers. I was young, enthu-
siastic, and naive. After the conclusion of one such negotiation, the dealer and I shook hands, drank the ritual
cups of tea, and were, I felt, the best of friends. I took the
official company agency agreement out of my case and
started to fill in the figures, preparatory to signing it.
"Why are you doing that?" asked the dealer in some
alarm. "If you think that I am going to sign that you are
much mistaken." "But I am only writing in the figures
which we agreed on." "If we agreed to them, why do you
want a legal document? It makes me suspect that you
have got more out of this agreement than I have, and are
going to use the weight of the law to enforce your terms.
In my culture," he went on, "a good agreement is self-
enforcing because both parties go away smiling and are
happy to see that each other is smiling. If one smiles and

the other scowls, the agreement will not stick, lawyers or no lawyers."

I think that I persuaded him that it was just a piece of company ritual and of no significance, but the episode got me thinking. I had grown up in a culture which believed that a good negotiation was one in which only one party, myself, came away smiling, but concealed that smile lest the other guess that one had gotten the better of him or her. Negotiation was about winning. You then had to enforce your side of the deal, using the law or the threat of the law. I had met a culture where negotiation was about finding the best way forward for both parties. No wonder we needed so many lawyers in our culture.

The Chinese contract, I later realized, embodied a principle that went far beyond the making of lasting commercial deals. It was about the importance of compromise as a prerequisite of progress. Both sides have to concede for both to win. It was about the need for trust and a belief in the future. Writ large, it was about sacrifice, the willingness to forego some present good to ward off future evil, or, more positively, it was about investment—spending now in order to gain later.

We have no chance of managing the paradoxes if we are not prepared to give up something, if we are not willing to bet on the future, and if we cannot find it in ourselves to take a risk with people. These are our pathways through the paradoxes if we have the will. The pursuit of our own short-term advantage, and the desire to win everything we can, will only perpetuate animosities, destroy alliances and partnerships, frustrate progress, and breed lawyers and the enforcement bureaucracy.

The Chinese contract, as I discovered to my chagrin, involves a major rethinking of our cultural habits, even in China, where they may not appreciate my magnification of their trading habits into a principle of life. The pursuit of self-interest has to be balanced, as Adam Smith's two books remind us, by "sympathy," a fellow feeling for others which is, he argues, the real basis of moral behavior. Only if we are conditioned by this sympathy will we want to take risks with our fellow men and women, will we trust them, or want to make life better for those we never meet. As Arthur Okun put it: "the 'invisible hand' needs to be accompanied by an 'invisible handshake.'" Unbalanced self-interest can only lead to an environment in which any victory will mean destroying those on whom our own survival will ultimately depend. That would be, literally, the paradox to end all paradoxes. The tragedy of the commons, it was labeled, when individual farmers maximized their own short-term use of the common land only to find that, when everyone did the same, the land deteriorated until all grazing failed.

There are those who think that sympathy will always be a very weak force, always yielding to self-interest. The evidence, however, is against them. Jean Piaget studied young children at play, and observed an inherent sense of fairness, particularly in older children who had longer time horizons. "It makes her happy," or "I don't want to see him cry," were the common explanations for gifts of generosity, and there was more generosity than there was hoarding. The Chinese will be relieved. Their policy of one child per family means that all young children spend their early years without siblings. The Chinese have, therefore, started courses in sharing in the primary schools—to help them learn the principle of the Chinese contract! Adults don't always lose the habit. Most people don't jack up the price of candles in a power strike or shovels in a snowstorm. There is sympathy in humankind as well as greed and cruelty.

THE MORALITY OF COMPROMISE

The "morality of compromise" sounds contradictory. Compromise is usually a sign of weakness, or an admission of defeat. Strong men don't compromise, it is said, and principles should never be compromised. I shall argue, conversely, that strong men know when to compromise and that all principles can be compromised to serve a greater principle. I have said "strong men" because I am assured that strong women have always known the value of compromise in the interests of progress.

Most of the dilemmas that we face in this time of confusion are not the straightforward ones of choosing between right and wrong, where compromise would, indeed, be weakness, but the much more complicated dilemmas of right and right. I want to spend more time on my work, *and* with my family; we want to be good corporate citizens *and* return a decent profit; we want to trust our subordinates *but* we need to know what they are doing. At other times, the interests of different parties are in conflict. Without compromise by both there will be no movement. Stalled by a refusal to make concessions, the place stagnates. Progress is sacrificed to pride.

I once listened to Lord Owen, then Dr. David

Owen. He had just finished his stint as foreign secretary in Britain's Labour Government of the 1970s and was not yet the leader of the Social Democrats. He was addressing a group of bishops on a topic of his own choosing—the morality of compromise. He had, he said, one August, while on his own in the Foreign Office, when most of the staff were on holiday, received a request to provide riot and control equipment to the Shah of Iran, whose regime was fast falling apart. The Shah and his regime were deeply repugnant to him, they offended all the principles of democracy and social justice in which he and his party believed. Nevertheless, as he weighed the alternatives, with no one around to give advice, he concluded that to meet the request was preferable to the only alternative, a shoot-out by the Shah's army with dead bodies in the street. He gave support to a regime he abhorred because the alternative was worse. One principle was sacrificed to a greater principle.

If you stick too fast to your position, he told the bishops, you may be comforted by feeling that you are in the right, but you may also have committed the greater wrong of stalling any movement in what is generally the right direction. It is ironic that, some years later, it was David Owen's too-rigid adherence to his own position that helped precipitate the demise of the party he led. Years later, he found himself trying to persuade Serbians, Bosnians, and Croatians to compromise in order to move forward, toward peace in the old Yugoslavia.

Peter and Pam Richards grow fruit and vegetables on their farm in the Channel Islands. The market is very competitive and life is not easy. They are also members of The Friends of the Earth, and ecological enthusiasts. "But," says Peter, "if we did not cover our new potatoes with polythene they would be ruined in two weeks." "We have had to learn to balance our idealism with pragmatism," said Pam, "to compromise. I suppose," she added, "that it's part of growing up!"

There is, however, a seductive power in certainty. If you have no doubts, then you never see the need to compromise. Unprincipled people are not, in fact, unprincipled. They have, instead, one overriding principle, which may be self-interest, or the good of the business or the nation as they see it, or even what they might call "the will of God." These principles they will not compromise. There will be no way forward with them, except on their chosen road and in their chosen vehicle. Their certainty gives them power, but at a cost. There is no room for anyone else in their camp, except for converts. Such people never see the need for a second curve, and, in time, their curve turns down. The certainty and self-assurance of a good leader must be tempered with the spirit of compromise if others are not to feel excluded. Margaret Thatcher was one who never felt the need to compromise. Her certainty gave her strength, and was much admired, even by those who disapproved of what she did with it, but in the end, the refusal to compromise brought her down. Compromise is essential to democracy. It is also essential to leaders who want willing and able followers, not sycophants.

Yet excessive compromise can give away too much. It can be seen as weakness, not as consensus building. The wrong compromise can block progress, not promote it. Like many people, I hate conflict. I shrink from confrontation. To avoid it, I am prone to give anything away. To escape the inevitable conflict I have refrained from removing people who were, by their incompetence, I knew, harming the organization. I have been tempted to let a bullying neighbor have his way rather than confront him. That is bad compromise, compromise for the wrong reason. I was compromising the truth for the sake of a quiet life, a minor principle for a greater one. It should be the other way around, as I well knew.

Arriving at one management program, the executives found an English translation of Sophocles' Greek tragedy *Antigone* on their desks. This was their first homework of the course. They thought at first that they had been mixed up with liberal arts students, but they realized the point of it when they started to talk about the play as a group. Antigone's brother had been defeated and killed by their uncle, Kreon, in a battle for the control of Thebes. He had been left outside the city walls to be picked at by the vultures. Antigone's faith required her to see that her brother was properly buried, lest he be pursued forever by the Furies. Kreon forbade it, on pain of her death. Do you obey authority, or do you do what you think is right, come what may? Or do you find a compromise? It has been the dilemma of conquered peoples down through the ages. It is a conflict not unknown in businesses, or even in families. Antigone stuck to her principles, and died for them. There *are* some principles worth dying for. The question is—was this one of them? It is because that question is forever topical that the play is still performed 2,500 years later.

Only when the compromise is in pursuit of a greater purpose, or a greater principle, is it right to compromise a principle. As well as conflict, I abhor war and violence. But there are bullies, and there are bully states, who respect only those who are stronger than they and who are prepared to show it. Therefore, I will condone limited war and the controlled use of force in pursuit of peace and order if all else fails. I will even fight myself if the cause is just. To stick too tightly to my principles would be to give in to all bullies and all criminals. The greater principle of a just order legitimizes the abandonment of a lesser principle.

Most compromise in life, however, is not about our principles but about our interests. No compromises on these can ultimately mean no allies, and no progress. The philosophy of Chinese contracts can then prove more fruitful if less glorious.

CONTRACTS WITH THE FUTURE

Time also demands its compromises, as we try to balance the demands of the present and the future. Short-termism is an ugly word for a tough dilemma. Businesses are accused of it, governments are plagued by it, none of us can escape it in our own lives. We all live with the knowledge that the things which we want most, and which are best for us—health, affection, long life—require us to give up immediate delights or to do things we'd rather not do. Personal short-termism damages our health. We know, in other words, that this sort of personal compromise is one way of dealing with the paradox that most of the things we enjoy are bad for us.

The dilemma is this—to what extent should you short-change or compromise the present in order to benefit the future? All investment involves taking something from today to improve tomorrow. It only makes sense to do that if you believe in, or want, what tomorrow may bring. It is always another compromise. To what extent are we prepared to curb our bad environmental habits to ensure a cleaner, safer world for our grandchildren, a world which we may not live long enough to enjoy? To what extent will we curb our own behavior if others do not do likewise? Will the tragedy of the commons be played out on a global scale or will we adjust our short-term behavior for a greater common cause, to make life better for people we shall never meet? We will only do it, I believe, if we can look beyond the grave, if we can accept that there are some things that are more important than ourselves, and longer lasting.

At a more personal level, young dual-career couples struggle with this issue of common cause and compromise as they try to decide whether or when to start a family. The sacrifices in the present will be considerable, a loss of income, a change of life-style, an altered relationship. The commitment of both of them to a new future is critical, if they are to make the necessary compromises to start another family. It is, however, an impossible decision to make if they want to preserve their present while growing that future. They have to start by understanding that compromise is essential to most progress, but that voluntary compromise is only possible if there is a common cause, a cause greater than oneself, and a trust in the other. When compromise goes out of fashion among the young, so do babies.

In a business, to increase a dividend is to reduce the sums available for new capital spending. If the shareholders are not interested in the future of the company because they can sell their shares tomorrow, they will want to see dividends, not retained profits, in the accounts. The managers, on the other hand, with their own futures linked to that of the business, will want to invest as much as they can in that future. There can often be a conflict of priorities.

If there is no common cause, no agreement on the longer-term goal, the more pressing priority, or the most powerful party, will win out. If we think that we need shareholders more than managers, as we seem to, the shareholders will win. Compromise will be enforced, not voluntary—a British contract rather than a Chinese one. Only if the shareholders are also locked into the future of the business, as shareholders more often are in Japan and Germany, will they have common cause with the managers and be prepared to forego some present gains for future profits. As long, that is, as that common cause seems a worthwhile one. In the end, for the long term to prevail over the short term, we must want what the long term promises. Where there is no vision, there you find short-termism, for then there is no reason to compromise today for an unknown tomorrow.

The concept of stock options, common in Britain and America, is an attempt to make common cause between senior managers and the shareholders. The thinking is that they will tie the managers' compensation more closely to the longer-term performance of the company. It does, but it is because the managers can only make use of those options after a period of years or if the share price goes higher than the price of the options. If all shareholders were treated this way, they would look at the company a little differently. It would significantly alter the balance between the present and the future and so make compromise easier.

THE THIRD
ANGLE

If we want self-reinforcing relationships, Chinese contracts, we need to find a common cause, one that justifies some personal sacrifice by both parties for a greater common good. Without that sense of common cause, everyone will fight their own corner, trust between individuals or groups will be rare, and compromise will be something imposed on the weaker by the stronger, a sign of defeat not progress. In a democratic culture, if it is not to degenerate into a battle between interest groups, it is particularly crucial that we find that common cause.

Where there is a third corner, we can often agree to combine our individual corners against the common enemy, realizing that we have more to gain by combining than by standing alone. The value of the compromise seems self-evident. Fighting a common enemy, however, results in temporary alliances because the compromise was made on the assumption that the enemy would be defeated. When the defeat occurs, the alliance evaporates. If, on the other hand, the enemy continues to resist defeat, the compromises made for the alliance begin to be questioned when there is no payoff. When businesses define their purpose as being bigger or better than a competitor in the hope that this will unite their workforces, they are playing short-term games. When the British government sets its sights on outperforming Germany or France, it is playing games too long to be real.

A common enemy is seldom a good reason for a lasting compromise or for long-term sacrifice, except in times of real, not economic war, times which, we must hope, will seldom come. In many a situation there is, however, a third angle, a way of finding that balance between opposites which is a necessary pathway through paradox.

The year 1793 was the bicentenary of one of the most influential graffiti of all time. On June 30 of that year, the Club des Cordeliers of Paris passed a resolution that all house owners should be invited to paint on the facades of their houses, in big letters, these words: "Unite, indivisibilité de la République, Liberté, Egalité, Fraternité ou la Mort." It was the first recorded example of what was to be the motto of the French revolution—Liberty, Equality, and Fraternity. It was also the best-known example of trinitarian thinking, the "third term" that reconciles opposites. Liberty, notoriously, cancels out equality, and vice versa. The two can only survive in any sort of harmony if there is fraternity. If we care for one another, we will not press our demands for individual liberty so far that it intrudes on your equal right to be free, nor will your pressure for equality be pushed so far that it denies me my liberty.

Most of life is made up of opposites—male and female, work and leisure, life and death. In the British tradition, it is always assumed that a conflict between opposites is the best recipe for fairness. The system of justice is based on this assumption, as is the British Parliament. In the view of many it is neither fair nor always just.

Trinitarian, or third-angle, thinking is always looking for solutions which can reconcile or illuminate the opposites. A third party may yet be the answer to the seesaw of British politics, a seesaw that periodically gets jammed so that one party stays in power too long for fairness. An independent assessor in the judicial process may yet emerge as a solution to the battle of the courtrooms where victory for one side or the other is not always the same as justice. A common humanity is the concept which makes sense of the conflict between male and female. If we knew better what we meant by eternity, we might not see life and death as such polar opposites. Learning might be a way of linking work and leisure so that they blend into one another. Love quenches rows and turns differences into stimulants, and sympathy, Adam Smith would remind us, makes the market moral.

Trinitarian thinking urges us always to be on the lookout for another approach, a third angle. Trinitarian thinking says that if money is so divisive, why not demonetarize society. If more of the good or necessary things in life were free to all, like education, housing, health care, travel, and essential foods, there would be more equality. It would be less easy to distinguish between rich and poor, and there would be less reason to pile up riches. Trinitarian thinking suggests that if the struggle between owners and workers is endemic, we could get around it by thinking of both as members.

I remember only too well the arguments with my two children over the telephone. We tried budgets, time limits, locks, and total prohibition as ways to curb their insatiable appetite for telephoning their friends as teenagers. The only results were evasion, lies, and rows. Trinitarian thinking suggested another route. I paid for each of them to have their own telephone and for the basic charge, provided they paid for all their calls. If the bills were not paid, they got cut off. My phone would not then, or ever, be available. They saw this as freedom, but I noticed that, from then on, it was their friends, no doubt using their parents' phones, who phoned them! My hugely reduced bills more than compensated for the extra basic charges; besides, I now had unrestricted access to my own telephone! It was a compromise which worked without any sacrifice of principle.

In one condominium, the problems of parking were the hardest problem to solve. It was seen as a basic right to be able to park your car, and that of your visitors, outside your apartment. On the other hand, no one wanted to have their view interrupted by other people's cars. Endless arrangements and architectural devices were explored but no one was satisfied. Trinitarian thinking suggested that the fairest solution would be a communal parking site away from all the apartments, to declare the main area a car-free site and to landscape it appropriately. Some shared inconvenience became a small price to pay for enhanced beauty and peace. Another compromise which worked because we found the third angle. Shrewd negotiators know all about such unblocking, trinitarian devices.

This book will contain many examples of trinitarian thinking. It is often a path to acceptable compromise. However we get there, we need more Chinese contracts in our lives, in our businesses, and in our societies. The Japanese are famed for the slowness of their decision making but also for the strength and reliability of those decisions once made. The reason, as we know, is the length of time it takes to reach a consensus among all the parties involved. You could say that the Chinese contract is a Japanese habit! The rest of us could learn it to advantage, but that will mean changing some of our cultural traditions: the idea, for instance, that winning necessarily means that someone loses, instead of the possibility that all can win a little less, that compromise is a sign of weakness not of strength, that a good lawyer is better than a good agreement, and that if you look after the present, the future will take care of itself. These things are culturally determined, they are not engrained in human nature. We can change the way we think.

The starting premise of this book was that there is no perfect solution to anything, and that no one can predict the ultimate effect of any action with any certainty. Only when you look back can you see the truth. Even science knows no perfect answers, nor believes that there can be any. Given this premise, one would have to be very arrogant, very stupid, or very insensitive to claim to know the complete truth of anything in advance. Karl Popper once said, "We all differ in what we know, but in our infinite ignorance we are all equal." Even popes can be wrong, which won't stop them or others from seeking to impose their wishes on the world. They have that right.

We all have the right to think that we are right, because the good news from that starting premise is that there is room for each one of us to make a difference. Fluttering our wings, we, like the butterfly, may upset the weather. When no one knows the future with any certainty, we have the right to dream. But for anyone's wishes or dreams to be accepted without enforcement, some form of Chinese contract will be necessary, one in which the interests of all parties, both now and in the future, are heard and heeded.

That is a hard, even paradoxical, message. In turbulent times we look for certainty and sure authority. We want to be followers, not leaders, even in a small way. We want "them" to solve our dilemmas, and give us back a quiet life. It is hard enough to look after oneself without taking other people into account. I am arguing that these things cannot and will not be. The paradoxes are too complicated. We have to get involved if there is to be any point to our existence. We have to put these principles into practice, in our work and in our lives. That is the concern of the next part of the book.

Practicing the Preaching

Managing Paradox

The Federal Idea

THE FEDERAL IDEA

Different cultures give a different prominence to the idea of the individual, but one can sense a growing feeling of impotence, everywhere, in the face of institutions and government, local and global. Democracy used to mean that the people had the power, but now that translates into the people have the vote, which is not the same thing. The vote is an expression of last resort, a useful reminder to our rulers of the source of their bread and butter, but hardly a way for individuals to influence what is going on around them. Moreover, in the institutions of everyday life, particularly those of business, the only people with the vote are those outside, the financiers or the governors. Those who work in them are effectively disenfranchised. Democracy has its limits.

If we want to reconcile our humanity with our economics, we have to find a way to give more influence to what is personal and local, so that we can each feel that we have a chance to make a difference, that we matter. We have no hope of charting a way through those paradoxes unless we feel able to take some personal responsibility for events. A formal democracy will not be enough. We have to find another way, by changing the structure of our institutions to give more power to the small and to the local. We have to do that, with all the untidiness which it entails, while looking for efficiency, and the benefits of coordination and control. But more is needed than good intentions to empower the individual to do what we want him or her to do. The structures and the systems have to change to reflect a new balance of power. That means federalism.

Federalism is an old idea, but its time may have come again because it matches paradox with paradox. Federalism seeks to be both big in some things and small in others, to be centralized in some respects and decentralized in others. It aims to be local in its appeal and in many of its decisions, but national or even global in its scope. It endeavors to maximize independence, provided that there is a necessary interdependence; to encourage difference, but within limits; it needs to maintain a strong center, but one devoted to the service of the parts; it can, and should, be led from that center but has to be managed by the parts. There is room in federalism for the small to influence the mighty, and for individuals to flex their muscles.

We think of federalism as applying to countries—the United States, Germany, Switzerland, Australia, Canada. Her politicians might not admit it, but the United Kingdom is really a federation of its separate regions, as is Spain, and, increasingly, even France, as its regions gain more autonomy. The concept, however, goes beyond countries. Every organization of any size can be thought of in federal terms. Hospitals, schools, local government, and most charities are, if we look at them with federal spectacles, made for federalism, local and separate activities bonded in one whole, served by a common center. All businesses of any size have federal propensities, and a need to be all the things which federalism offers.

Why has such a good idea not been so obviously popular? Few businesses are consciously federal, nor does history provide many, if any, examples of a monarch or a central power voluntarily moving to a federalist structure. The hard truth is that we are always reluctant to give up power unless we have to, and federalism is an exercise in the balancing of power. The federal idea is an example of the second curve, but one which too few institutions or societies develop until they are forced to. It is a very different, and very uncomfortable, way of thinking about organizations. It is messy, untidy, and always a little out of control. Its only justification is that there is no real alternative in a complicated world. No one person, or group, or executive, is so all-wise and so all-sensitive to be able to balance the paradoxes on their own, or run the place from the center, even if people were prepared to allow them to. We have to allow space for the small and the local.

Federalism relies on a set of Chinese contracts between its various parts and operates through doughnuts of varying size and shape, which leave, of necessity and of right, considerable space for local decisions. The goals of the parts have to adjust to the requirements of the whole, and vice versa. No one in a federal organization can have everything exactly as they want it. Therefore, it is an excellent example of putting the preaching of this book into practice, with all its difficulties as well as opportunities.

Let us be clear, federalism is not the easiest of concepts to make work, or to understand. Yugoslavia is hardly an advertisement for the concept, nor is Canada. California is creaking under an excess of federalism from within and without. IBM proclaims its conversion to the idea, but may not be its most successful exponent in the years ahead. A federal Europe frightens many, and not just in Britain. Nevertheless, we have to persevere because it is the best way to return some sense of meaning to our larger institutions, a way of connecting their purposes with their people.

Much of the confusion and difficulty arises from a misunderstanding of what federalism is. A confederation, for example, is not the same thing as a federation. A confederation is an alliance of interested parties who agree to do some things together. It is a mechanism for mutual advantage. There is no reason for sacrifice or trade-offs or compromise unless it is very obviously in one's own interest. A confederation is not an organization that is going anywhere, because there is no mechanism or will to decide what that anywhere might be. The Confederation of Independent States, which replaced the Soviet Union, will never be an effective body. The British Commonwealth, another confederation, is a thing of sentiment and language, not a real organization. These are not the stuff of federalism.

Confederations adapt when they have to, usually too late. They do not lead, nor do they build. They are organizations of expediency, not of common purpose. The British would like Europe to remain an economic confederation, a common market. Many in the rest of Europe want a more federal state, one with a greater common purpose, within which sacrifices and compromises are acceptable, one in which the rich are readier to help the poorer, one with common standards and common aspirations.

What is true of Europe is also true of organizations. Alliances, joint ventures, and networks are the tools of confederations, arrangements of mutual convenience, inevitably fragile as the conveniences change. Organizations with a clear purpose will want to be federal, not confederal. The distinction is important.

The key concepts in federalism are *twin citizenship and subsidiarity.* They are old ideas, re-invented for today's world.

6 *Twin Citizenship*

The Texan, when I visited him, was very obviously a Texan, and proud of it. On his front lawn there was a tall white flagpole flying the Stars and Stripes. "Why not," he said, in response to my query. "I'm an American, aren't I?" He was American *and* he was Texan.

BIG BUT

SMALL

Twin citizenship is a critical component of federalism: you belong to your own state and to the larger federal union of states. Each of us will probably have a number of twin citizenship situations in our lives. It is important that we do. Even in personal life one has twin loyalties more often than not. When I married, I thought that I was joining two lives together, mine and that of the girl I loved. It was only when we started to arrange the wedding that I realized that I was also becoming the affiliated member of a new tribe, her large and extended family. I now had my tribe and hers, twin citizenships and twin loyalties to be reconciled and balanced. Organizations, for their part, are going federal, just as countries have, because they want to give a measure of independence to local units or to specialized groups. At the same time, they want to retain the benefits of scale. Being big and small makes sense, but managing it creates problems.

Small units are faster, more focused, more flexible, more friendly, and more fun—to borrow Rosabeth Moss Kanter's five f's. Small units can get closer to the customer and the citizen, to the patient or to the student. They can be less bureaucratic and more personal. Most of us frogs prefer a smaller pond, if the truth be told. In smaller groups there is more chance to be yourself, less likelihood of being anonymous.

On the other hand, there are always economies of scale to be had in any organization. They are most easily found in finance, distribution, and purchasing, less often, these days, in manufacturing. Research, if it is any good, is increasingly expensive. Pharmaceutical companies have to be large, as do oil companies and airplane makers. Large organizations offer better hopes of security to their people, more variety, and more scope. They can afford to invest in the kind of fundamental training which takes years to pay off. "Now that you've been with us for ten years," my oil company told me, "you may be worth your keep!" Many worry that if the BBC in Britain were to turn itself into a host of mini-independents, there would be no one interested in paying for the professional training which will groom the directors and technicians of the future.

Federalism is an age-old device for keeping the proper balance between big and small. Big in some things, small in others. It is never easy, because it means allowing the small to be independent while still being part of the larger whole, to be different but part of the same. Federalism is fraught with difficulty because it is trying to manage the paradox. Twin citizenship makes that possible. If there is the sense of belonging to something bigger as well as to something smaller, we can accept some restrictions on our local independence if it helps the larger whole. Sovereignty is not ceded but shared. The larger unit is not only "them" but also "us."

To many British, Europe has always been a place one went to, not a place one belonged to. Until they instinctively realize that they are in it, geographically as well as politically, Europe and the European Community will remain "them," not "us." They will not have a sense of twin citizenship and a gut feeling for federalism, which will remain a synonym for a loss of independence without a compensating new belonging.

Local citizenship is the easy part. We can all identify with our immediate neighbors, particularly when we are also working with them. Our futures depend on them. We share a history, we know their faces, often too well, and we know where we belong. As an old Chinese proverb has it, those who do not know the village they have come from, will never find the village they are looking for. Richard Rogers, the architect who designed the Pompidou Centre in Paris and the Lloyd's building in London, commented that Europe is becoming increasingly defined by its cities. Barcelona's Olympics were about Barcelona not Spain. Dresden is intent on being, once again, a center of culture, art, and education, a place for Europe, not just Germany. We can relate to our cities more easily than we can to the idea of Europe, or America.

It is that larger citizenship which is harder to establish, yet it needs equal prominence if there is to be a proper balance. In a business, it may be logical to combine functions, to group some regions together, to manage cash or purchasing centrally, but these actions steal power and decisions from independent units. Those units will be resentful, not understanding the paradox that in order to get the most value out of their independence it often pays to sacrifice some of that independence to a central function. That kind of compromise is only done willingly if there is confidence in the central function, a sense of belonging to a larger whole. We need that second citizenship.

THE £5
AUCTION

To prove this obvious point, I used to play a simple game with executives on training exercises. It was a variety of what logicians call the Prisoner's Dilemma, except that in my game I offered to auction three £5 notes between two participants. I would place two volunteers in chairs facing away from one another so that they could not see the other's face. I asked them to bid in turn for the first note. Invariably the first person bid £1, the second upped it, and so it went on, by alternative bids, sometimes going up by £1, sometimes jumping by £2, sometimes by parts of a pound, until one of them reached £5 at which point the other normally, but not always, stopped bidding. In one case, someone actually bid £23 for the first £5 note! The auction for the second note gave first bid to the other side but the outcome was the same—£5 or more bid for my £5 note. So it was for the third note, although there was often overbidding for this note, too, so that one side could claim a sort of Pyrrhic victory—more notes won, and to hell with the cost!

The rest of the group watched, amazed by the apparent idiocy of the bidding. There would be a rush of volunteers for the next round, eager to try out their theory of preemptive bidding. The result would be the same as long as I was careful to pick them from different sides of the room. Finally, I would choose a couple who had been sitting and whispering together and who volunteered in unison. When they started the bidding, the first person would bid 10 pence and the second would say "no bid." The note had been sold for 10p. The same happened the other way around with the second note. Bidding for the third note was more tense. Usually their agreement held. The first person bid the now standard 10p. and the other passed. At the end, they took the three £5 notes, paid me 30p., and shared the proceeds. Occasionally, however, competition flared up again for the final note and the second bidder would come in with a preemptive £5 bid. They would then have to make do with a £4 80p. profit instead of £14-70p. and live with a sense of betrayal.

What was going on? I would ask the group. Logical,

sensible, mature individuals were competing to the point of lunacy because I had kept them apart. By not allowing them to communicate, I had also prevented them from establishing an alliance, an agreed-on objective, and a means of proceeding. Only when I picked people who had had a chance to talk together were they able to achieve a common goal which benefited them both, although even that broke down on occasion. A common cause, the willingness to deny oneself in the interests of that common cause, and trust that the other party will do the same—these are the essentials of sensible organizational behavior. Much of the time this sensible behavior does not happen because people do not talk, do not trust, and have no common cause. To put it more crisply, there is no sense of a second citizenship, and therefore no possibility of sensible compromise.

The depressing thing was that the experiment never failed. It always worked the way I knew it would. We instinctively work for our own immediate advantage unless there is an obvious common cause with people whom we can trust so that an initial sacrifice turns out in the end to be to our mutual advantage. Today, we can see the £5 auction game being played for real around the world.

THE QUEEN'S GREAT MATTER

The second citizenship is critical. Interestingly, politicians and managers both use the same sort of devices to re-inforce that larger loyalty. They make sure there is a federal flag, or company logo, which is displayed wherever and whenever possible. They have national anthems, or vision and value statements in organizations, things more symbolic than real but important nonetheless because they give expression to the ideal which holds the whole together, the sense of common cause to which we are, they hope, committed.

Modern organizations spend a lot of time working on that common cause, establishing what it is, communicating it, re-inforcing it. It can look like waffle, and it sometimes is. Properly done, it is not waffle but the glue of the enterprise. More respectfully, Richard Pascale and Anthony Athos call it the "spiritual fabric" of the corporation. They are describing companies in present-day Japan. The tradition is older still. In Elizabethan England they called it the Queen's Great Matter, the common cause that bonded her merchant venturers and built an empire. In America, every president goes out of his way, in his inaugural address, to emphasize that he will govern for all his fellow citizens, not just the ones who voted for him. He points out that they can only help themselves if they also help each other. He reminds his audience that there is this tradition called America, which they need to rediscover. "We must prove that we deserve our heritage." This is not empty rhetoric but the necessary forging of a common purpose. Sadly, the rhetoric too easily gets lost in the day-to-day reality. Living up to the rhetoric of the larger citizenship is one of the toughest parts of leadership.

Presidents, leaders, to be effective have to represent the whole to the parts and to the world outside. They may live in the center but they must not *be* the center. To

re-inforce the common cause they must be the chief missionary, ever traveling, ever talking, ever listening. This
role sits ill with that of chief executive, which is why
many organizations are now separating the two roles.
The missionary task is not a role easily fulfilled by committee or by memorandum because logic makes few
hearts beat faster and no one has ever followed a committee into battle. The life of the federal president in a large
organization tends to be one long teach-in. Successful
presidents and prime ministers know that their main task
is to carry the people with them. Roosevelt with his fireside radio talks, Clinton with his town meetings,
Churchill and his wartime broadcasts were all, in effect,
running popular teach-ins.

Twin citizenship needs more than flags, national anthems, and articulate, visible leaders. It is lubricated by
cross-fertilization, by moving people between the parts
and between the parts and the center. In that way more
people are exposed to more of the bigger reality; they
not only grow themselves but their vision and understanding of the total organization grow with them. Shell,
one of the oldest of the corporate federations, knows that
its corps of 5,000 expatriates is the bond that holds it all
together, far more than any shareholdings or formal au-
thorities. On a different scale, Club Med, another federal
organization with its independent holiday centers, insists
that site managers change locations every two or three
years, creating an international family of shared habits
and values.

A common legal framework and a common currency are the other essentials. They both remind everyone, constantly, that they are part of something bigger. That is their symbolic role; they also have a practical one, to allow the parts to work together.

A common legal framework translates, in organizations, into a basic set of guidelines—"how we do things around here." They call it the "bible" in some places, but they would be wise not to make it as bulky or as subject to devious interpretation as the Bible proper. Too much law only breeds lawyers, who come expensive. A common currency translates into a common information system so that inputs and outputs can be measured and compared across the parts. That sounds like common sense were it not so uncommon. Too often the sales department talks of sales but knows not what contribution it makes to added value, while purchasing talks costs but knows not what difference they make to sales. In the past, in Britain, when doctors prescribed drugs or referred their patients to specialists, they neither knew nor thought it right to know what these cost. They felt that to know would have influenced their medical judgment. They then complained that the funds to cure the sick were never adequate. In the National Health Service at that time there was no common currency and, therefore, no sense of involvement in, or responsibility for, the financial aspects of the organization. Paradoxically, by breaking down the health-care system into more self-accountable units, the sense of common cause has become stronger because the parts now have to talk to one another and have the means to do it. As they say, an organization that talks together stays together.

Yet we must take care that the laws and the currency are not so pervasive that they swamp local citizenship. The center may yearn for uniformity, for an identikit organization in which every bit is the same as every other bit, but the customer or client wants it to be his or her preference at the point of delivery, and the local unit wants to be able to be appropriately different. Uniformity, like equality, is the enemy of liberty, but too much liberty can destroy efficiency. There has to be a balance.

Our new local superstore does not stock risotto rice. That product might be thought exotic in an out-of-the-way corner of England but I delight in the infinite variety that is possible with this simplest of ingredients. I spoke with the store manager about stocking it. He was regretful, but the shelf layout and the stocklist were decided on at the center and he had no discretion. How, I wondered, could the center be so all-knowing as to discern the rich randomness of tastes in our neck of the woods, or did they not trust him? What, if any, discretion was he allowed in other areas, or was he but a walking automaton, there to give standard nonresponses to queries like mine? There was little sense of local citizenship there. An identikit, facsimile organization imposes uniformity on its world, thinks that the center knows best, that discretion is dangerous, and that local differences are unnecessary. All those assumptions, I suggest, are dangerous because they deny the paradoxes, they bury them instead of balancing them.

We would be wise, too, to remember another lesson from my auction game. Money talks. Money may not be the most important thing in the world but it provides the counters. Twin citizenship is much easier to believe in if there is some financial involvement in both citizenships. Without the tokens the game may not seem real. Our pay is beginning to reflect this. Profit-sharing schemes are not as rare as they once were. They may go further still. The time will come when an individual will find that annual pay comes in four lumps. The largest lump will be the pay for the job, reflecting one's standing in the organization, one's level of experience, expertise, and previous record as well as the level or grade of job. That is not new. What would be new, except in Japan, is that this lump might be only 50% of the total take-home pay in a good year. The other lumps would be a share in the overall surplus of the group or corporation, a share in the value-added by one's unit, the first citizenship, and, finally, a personal bonus reflecting one's individual contribution. The two shares might normally be expected to amount to 20% of the total package, leaving 10% for the individual contribution.

At first sight these numbers seem huge. Remember, however, that they start with a base salary or wage, which is set at 50% of normal take-home pay. That sum will not vary but the other numbers will, in line with actual performance. When times are good, the money will be good and there will be that much more to distribute because the basic costs are only half of what they could be. When times are hard, however, or performance slips, then total pay declines, but no one need be dismissed to reduce labor costs; they reduce automatically. In that way the obligations of citizenship are fulfilled: you keep your job and the rewards are shared when there are rewards to share. It is this kind of payment system that has helped Japanese companies to maintain lifetime employment for their key workers.

The percentages need to be big to be interesting. A total bonus element of 5% to 8%, the kind that some organizations play around with, does little more than pay for the Christmas or the New Year break. It is a gesture not a bond. The percentages must also be viewed as fair and objective. They must be based on real numbers, not on perceptions or judgments. The exception may be the percentage allowed for individual contribution. This can seldom be totally objective unless one is a salesperson on commission. Opinions have to count. The sense of local citizenship will be re-inforced if the opinions are those of the group itself, which is given a total sum of money to distribute among its members. A good, open group will not flinch from the task of allocating the money, accepting the fact that it will have to give reasons for giving anyone less or more than the mean. On the other hand, one's work group is not the only arbiter of one's contribution; superiors and colleagues outside the group have relevant opinions. Many a group will duck the issue and will parcel the money out equally. Balance is best. A bit of each also increases the opportunity for feedback. Critically, however, the individual element in the bonus should be less than the two group elements if the sense of twin citizenship is to be re-inforced.

Obviously, such a dramatic rearrangement of the reward system in an organization can only be instituted in one step on a greenfield site. Established organizations will have to do it gradually, taking full advantage of the good years to move forward faster, never forgetting the ultimate goal and being careful to explain, at all times, the why and what of it all. The system has to be seen as a way of sharing in the rewards of citizenship as well as in its risks.

THE DISAPPEARING MIDDLE

Twin citizenship implies that we are citizens of only two states. In theory there should be many more. I am a citizen of my town, then of my region, then of my country. Above and beyond that comes the trading bloc or the larger federal state and beyond that, why not, the world. Theory, however, does not always sit easily with psychological reality. Most of us seem to be capable of only two levels of loyalty in any one area of our lives. The ends of the chain often get dropped and the central levels get squeezed out. "I am a Scotsman first," my friend said, "and then a European. I don't feel British at all." Only those countries which are, like my Ireland, small enough to be tribes, do not get squeezed between the tribe and the federation. Businesses that try to put another layer of loyalty, often a geographical one, between the operating company and the corporate center, can confuse and weaken the sense of citizenship.

Governments, in their turn, have to decide which layer to omit in dispensing health, education, or welfare to their citizens. If they insist on retaining central control while delegating delivery to local units, the intermediary levels will only get in the way and atrophy. Either the national government has to devolve its power to the intermediary level, retaining only the roles of service and advice provider, with money allocated according to formula, or it turns the intermediary levels into optional resource centers for the units to draw on if they wish. Federalism then becomes a mechanism for centralization.

A more interesting example of the disappearing middle in government is suggested by David Osborne and Ted Gaebler in their book *Reinventing Government.* They want to see more of the ownership and control of public service institutions transferred from the bureaucrats and government professionals to communities and individuals. Citizen groups, neighborhoods, volunteer organizations would be authorized, and, where necessary, centrally funded, to carry out many of the local activities of government. If that were to happen, whole layers of administration would be unnecessary.

The new executive agencies in Britain are a step along this route. These are autonomous entities charged with the delivery of government services, ranging from the Benefit Agency to the central Office of Information. When they are truly autonomous, the federalism of government services will be well established. At present, the British Treasury is still reluctant to let go of all the strings. The pay and the grading and the numbers of staff, for instance, are centrally controlled. You cannot have a true feeling of local citizenship when you cannot determine your own staffing levels. Nor is the monitoring of technical details a substitute for the second and bigger loyalty, which will be essential if the old traditions of the Civil Service are not to get lost in the new proliferation of independent bodies. Federalism is not easy.

The state of California is fast becoming bogged down in too many layers of citizenship. It is hard to know where real responsibility lies, what with school and hospital boards, local communities, the state and the federal governments, and the continuing experiment with direct democracy whereby the voters can vote to turn specific propositions into law. Too many layers of citizenship is a bureaucratic nightmare, be it in a corporation or a country. More of the middle needs to disappear.

National parliaments in Europe's larger countries, themselves federations of tribal regions, know that they are likely to be squeezed out if and when Europe becomes a fuller federation. Understandably, they do not relish the thought. It is not nice to be a disappearing middle, even if a greater loyalty requires it. It is not only national parliaments that face this dilemma of the disappearing middle; organizational layers have been disappearing for a decade, not least because those organizations are re-organizing federally, even if they do not always call it that or recognize it as such. In the federal structure, hierarchies are limited and local; you relate to people in the wider organization because their roles are relevant to your needs, not because their status in the organization requires it. Forget the hierarchy, use the network.

I listened to the chairman of a large French supermarket and hotel chain explain his federal, devolved organization to a skeptical Spanish audience still hooked on hierarchy. "Please explain to us," one of them eventually asked in some frustration, "to whom does the manager of the store in Lyons report?" The chairman clearly did not understand the question: "Well," he said, "if it's a question of distribution, he will go to the expert who is, I think, in Marseilles, but if it is a purchasing problem, the right person is in Paris." "Yes, but who is his immediate boss?" "There isn't any one person whom he would call 'boss.'" You could see the mystification on the faces of the Spaniards who live in a partially federal country but do not, yet, run their organizations federally. Twin citizenship needs no middles.

THE LOSS
OF LOYALTY

Twin citizenship is key to one set of paradoxes, in our societies and in our organizations. By denying the local, smaller loyalty, we kill all liberty, incentive, and initiative and rely on the center to be right, as IBM did, to its great cost, in the early 1990s. By denying the bigger loyalty, inefficiencies, duplications, and misunderstandings will proliferate. We need both loyalties.

In 1993 the Social Affairs Unit of the British Home Office produced a book of essays entitled *A Loss of Virtue*, which argued that words like "duty," "loyalty," and "obligation" had disappeared from common usage. The authors blamed it on the growth of an amoral culture. Others attributed it to the failure of religion to cultivate a sense of right and wrong. Tony Blair, then the Labour

Party spokesman on Home Affairs, pointed out that the words had no meaning unless one felt that one belonged to something, something from which you could draw as well as give to. He was, in my words, saying that, without a sense of a second and a bigger citizenship, selfishness is inevitable. If we cannot create that feeling of a bigger citizenship in our people, there will be no balance in society and our language will, indeed, begin to change.

Federalism, properly understood, can restore that sense of a local belonging and a broader, bigger citizenship, in both our organizations and in society.

7 *Subsidiarity*

Subsidiarity is an ugly word. But once you have learned how to spell it and got your tongue around it, you will be unlikely to forget it. Subsidiarity is the idea at the core of federalism; it is the key element in learning; change, if it is to be effective, depends upon it; the work of teams requires it as does any attempt to make individuals take more responsibility for themselves. Yet it is a confusing word because it has nothing to do with subsidiaries.

REVERSE
DELEGATION

Jacques Delors once offered a prize for a good definition of this word. He need not have bothered, as various people were quick to remind him. Politically, the Tenth Amendment to the U.S. Constitution, laying down the principle of states' rights, does it, without using the actual word. Much earlier, the Roman Catholic Church, borrowing the idea from political theory, coined the word and turned it into a moral principle. It was last restated in a papal encyclical, "Quadragesimo Anno," in 1941: "It is an injustice, a grave evil and a disturbance of right order for a large and higher organization to arrogate to itself functions which can be performed efficiently by smaller and lower bodies . . ." Strong words. I translate them more simply: stealing people's responsibilities is wrong. You could also define subsidiarity as "reverse delegation"—the delegation by the parts to the center.

Not so long ago my young daughter started her own business with a partner. They had a good product, but they had never run a business before. As I watched them making what I was sure were dangerous and foolhardy decisions, the temptation to intervene and give them the benefit of my experience was overwhelming. I loved my daughter and I badly wanted her venture to succeed. I was bluntly told to mind my own business, not theirs. I realized, belatedly, that I was stealing her decisions, taking away their choices and their chance to claim success as their own or to learn from their failure. I apologized. Next time I would wait for them to ask for my advice— reverse delegation. I understood, then, why subsidiarity was a moral principle.

Federal organizations take subsidiarity seriously. They have to because they work on the principle of reverse delegation. The individual parts, or states, cede some of their powers to the center because they believe that the center can do some things better on a collective basis. Therefore, they retain as much independence as they think they can handle. These "reserve powers" of the center are negotiated jointly and then recorded in a formal constitution. All federal organizations have written constitutions. It may be that Britain's aversion to a written constitution has something to do with her intuitive distrust of federalism and its formality. There should be nothing vague or woolly about federalism or it gets cluttered up with overlapping responsibilities and misunderstandings.

As more and more organizations collect alliances around their cores, they are forced to negotiate what should be done by whom and pressured to allow as much discretion to the parts as is sensible and possible. What you do not own, you cannot dictate to; negotiation is inevitable, so is subsidiarity—leaving power as close to the action as possible.

THE NEW CENTER

Homa Bahrami, describing the new high-tech organizations of Silicon Valley, calls them multipolar, saying that they "are more akin to a federation or constellation of business units that are typically interdependent, relying on one another for critical expertise and know-how. They have a peer relationship with the center. The center's role is to orchestrate the broad strategic vision, develop the shared administrative and organizational infrastructure, and create the cultural glue which can create synergies." One company employs 100 professionals in corporate roles, including finance and administration, infrastructure support (which takes in purchasing), legal services, human resources, and corporate communications. All these roles, we should note, are service roles rather than decision-imposing roles.

The "horizontal organization" is also in fashion. As described by McKinsey consultants Ostroff and Smith, these organizations have ten key principles, including: "organize work around processes not functions and select key performance objectives, flatten hierarchy by minimizing non-added-value activities, make teams not individuals the principal building blocks of organizations." What they are saying is that the trick is to find the optimum level of subsidiarity and then collapse as much into that as possible, so that the group or team or individual have the means at their direct disposal to do what they are responsible for. In their view it is the team, which is close to the action, that is the appropriate level of subsidiarity. That done, it is the job of the center to set standards but not necessarily to specify how they should be met. The unit is then judged, after the event, by its performance against those objective standards. Some call this "process re-engineering," but that is only giving a modern name to an ancient principle, a principle that needs to be rediscovered if we are going to have any chance of coping with the turbulence of the times. No longer do people believe that the center or the top necessarily knows best; no longer can the leaders do all the thinking for the rest; no longer do people want them to.

Following this principle, organizations everywhere have been collapsing and dispersing their centers. The 100 professionals of Silicon Valley seem to be about standard. ABB, the Swedish-Swiss engineering giant, oversees 225,000 people with about that number in an undistinguished office building in Zurich. British Petroleum, in London, has twice that number but would like to reduce it. Richard Branson's Virgin empire makes do with five! One way organizations do it is by dispersing the center, spreading it around. There is no need to have all the people with responsibilities across the organization sitting in the same central place. Those who are responsible for coordinating a particular product range may sensibly be located where most of the work is done on that product. The research coordination can go to the biggest laboratory, a geographical watching brief to a country or state in that area. It spreads power around and down, giving those who are nearer to the action a sense of involvement, of ownership. It is subsidiarity in practice, as it is when the European Bank for Reconstruction and Development is located in London or the European University in Florence, or the European Parliament in Strasbourg. To put everything in Brussels would be to consolidate too much power in the center. It would be stealing responsibility.

Small the center should be, and partially dispersed, but it must be strong and well informed. After all, the center carries the ultimate responsibility for the whole. Its reserve powers typically include "new money," i.e., the choice of strategic investments; "new people," i.e., the right to make the key personnel decisions in the group; the design and management of the information system, which is the artery of the organization; and, most controversially, the "right of invasion" when things go wrong. Only those in the center have a view of the whole. They cannot run it, and should be too few in number to be tempted, but they can nudge, influence, and, if they have to, interfere. The center's principal task is to be the trustee of the future, but it needs to be sure that the present does not run out before the future arrives.

Federalism, insists Mike Bett of Britain's BT, cannot work without a strong center. In the past, this meant that a strong center was also a big one. A lot of people were needed to coordinate plans and monitor activities. Power was concentrated in one place; federalism existed in name only. The information revolution means that the center can now be well informed but small, it can be strong but dispersed. Power can be more balanced. The nerve center of the organization can be in the chief executive's laptop computer—and in several others simultaneously. "The Virtual Organization"—the image of the organization on your screen—is almost here, in our briefcases. The information age has made federalism possible.

This new, dispersed center has still, however, got to talk to itself as well as contemplate its screens. Videoconferences, voice mail, and other technological devices help, but there is no real substitute for looking someone in the eye while you talk or they talk. Dispersed centers mean a lot of travel and red-eyes. The physical centers of these dispersed organizations increasingly begin to resemble clubhouses, places where people meet, eat, and greet but do not do their daily work. Like a club, there is a resident staff, those corporate services listed above, for instance, but the key players in the organization live and work elsewhere and use the club for their necessary meetings. It is not even essential that the chairman or chief executive work out of the central club. For a large part of their time the officers will be out and about, with the troops, where the different decision centers are, teaching, coaching, looking, listening. When they do go to the club, they can even have their own up-market "puppy," or "cart," a mobile desk with electronic paraphernalia, which is wheeled out and plugged in whenever the owner checks in.

ITALIAN
STYLE

One begins to wonder, then, what will happen to the cathedrals of corporate power, the towering blocks which shape our skylines. It has often seemed strangely appropriate that the executive suite should be so high that it is, on occasion, above the clouds, but now that it is recognized that those in the center are not all-seeing we may find them coming, physically and metaphorically, closer to the ground. Will their old suites become apartments for rich geriatrics or will the whole edifice be razed? A changing skyline will be the outward sign of real subsidiarity.

The skylines of most Italian towns have not changed for centuries. It would, of course, be a cultural crime to tamper with the roofscapes of Siena or Florence, Rome, or Bologna; but I suspect that the organization of Italian society has something to do with it. In Italy, much to the frustration of its central government, real power still resides in the family and the local community. Subsidiarity has always bypassed the formal institutions of government. After I went to live, for part of the year, in Tuscany, I soon realized that there was no way that I could conform to the myriad Italian laws regulating the buildings you could build, the cars you could buy, the permits you should have, the taxes you ought to pay, the people you could employ, and the people you might allow to rent your home. Not only do the regulations change rather frequently, but the bureaucracy cannot cope with anyone, such as a law-abiding Anglo-Saxon, who wants to do it all by the book.

Nobody expects you to abide by the letter of every small regulation, but should you fall out with the local community, it has an array of laws to throw at you. The community where we live is a network of families. Everybody knows everybody, and knows what everybody is up to. You disregard the locals at your peril, with the law as a weapon only of last resort. Outsiders are welcomed but will never be insiders. Government can pontificate, legislate, and regulate but not to much effect. It is a very effective but informal system of local control.

Many would argue that subsidiarity has gone too far in Italy. The country is broke, and may, conceivably, be split into two or even three parts, while the locals seem to thrive. The mafia, the biggest of the families, still rules in some sections. Government is impotent, and has proved to be corrupt. The power has to be rebalanced if the country is to be a viable entity. This will only happen if there is a general recognition that some powers have to be ceded to the center for the good of all because federalism depends upon reverse delegation. This recognition is slowly dawning. The old politicians who let subsidiarity run riot, often to their own advantage, are on the way out. The balance will, I hope, be soon restored.

Italy is a land of families, of small units linked by networks, in business as well as life. What the Italians do instinctively, we must do deliberately. Subsidiarity means small units, small units with real responsibilities. Richard Branson likes units of 50 or 60, Antony Jay, in *Corporation Man*, favored 400 or 500 and provided compelling evidence from schools, Paris suburbs, and Australia. Bill Gates of Microsoft likes 200 as a maximum. Tom Peters has documented many cases of organizations like Union Pacific Railroad breaking themselves up into smaller units, in that case, of 600 people each, but comes down in favor of 150 as the natural size. He cites the findings in *New Scientist* magazine that "in most modern armies the smallest independent unit normally numbers 130–150 men," that "there is a critical threshold in the region of 150–200, with larger companies suffering a disproportionate amount of absenteeism and sickness," that "once an academic discipline becomes larger than (200 researchers) it breaks into two sub-disciplines," that "neolithic villages from the Middle East around 6000 BC typically seemed to have contained 120–150 people," and that "the Hutterites, contemporary North American fundamentalists, regard 150 as the maximum size for their communities."

Forget the precise size. The point is that we need the unit to be big enough to be competent to do what it has to do and small enough so that everyone knows everyone else in it. The Bishop of Occam would have understood. According to the principle of Occam's Razor, the unit should be as small as it can be and as large as it has to be, a paradox in balance.

SIGNATURES
AND ROWING EIGHTS

Subsidiarity, however, depends on a mutual confidence. Those in the center have to have confidence in the unit, while the unit has to have confidence in the center, and the members of the unit have to have confidence in one another. When mutual confidence exists there is no need for the books of procedures, the manuals, inspectors, performance numbers, and countersignatures that clutter up larger organizations. They are the signs of distrust, the atmosphere of fear that makes so many organizations seem like prisons for the human soul. They should not, need not, be like that. Our work can be our pride. Put it this way: we want to be able to sign our own work. A lot of people already figuratively do sign their work. Every member of the team that makes a television program has his or her name in the credits. As you watch the credits roll you wonder why anyone needs to know all those names. You don't need to know, but they need to tell you, they want the acknowledgment and the credit.

A friend was appointed manager of a small art-printing works. Shortly after his arrival he called the whole workforce together and told them that he was ashamed of the quality of much of the work that had been going out of the door. In the future, he told them, everyone who has worked on an order must sign their name on a slip that will go out with the order saying, "We are responsible for this work. We hope that you are pleased with it." "I expected a revolt," he said, "but instead they cheered." "We, too, have been ashamed of much of the work. But we thought that that was what you wanted—the lowest acceptable quality at the lowest cost. We are happy to sign our names, provided you supply us with the machines to allow us to do work to our standards." Subsidiarity depends on a mutual confidence, but putting your name to it is the best guarantee of quality that I know. It is the reason why professionals always sign their work. The signature acknowledges their responsibility. We know whom to blame if things go wrong—and whom to thank if they go right.

Such mutual confidence takes time to build up. It has to be earned by all concerned. I once described a typical British work team as being like a rowing eight— eight people going backward as fast as they can, without talking to each other, commanded by the one person who can't row. I thought that it was witty. I was quietly rebuked, afterward, by a member of the audience who happened to be an oarsman. "You couldn't be more wrong," he said, "to make fun of it. We couldn't go backward without talking or be content to be commanded by a nonrower if we did not know each other very well and have complete confidence in each other's ability to do the job they are supposed to do. That's why we practice together so much, eat together, and even live together for long periods."

I remembered, then, that Japanese groups are renowned for the time they spend together off the job, and I notice how actors not only rehearse but also socialize together. You have to know each other well, it seems, both on and off the job, to know whether you can have confidence, or more important, trust, in someone. My son had a typical British education, one designed to bring him out as an individual and to emphasize his personal qualities and skills. He stood out in a crowd. Then he went to drama school, where a group of 27 young people worked together, learning to perform plays, for three years. He quickly realized that he stood or fell according to the quality of the group as a whole. It is no use being a star in a mediocre team. He became a devoted groupie, teaching others what he knew and they didn't, and learning, in turn, new skills from them. Competition was out, cooperation was all. He had no time, he said, to see his other friends during the terms. The group came first. "We all depend upon each other." I accused him of going Japanese. That would be a compliment, he replied, because they understand what is needed in a group.

TOUGH
TRUST

Subsidiarity in a group sounds warm and reassuring. It is, in practice, tough, and has important consequences for those in charge. For one thing, the group has to be small enough and be together long enough for the mutual confidence to grow. Confidence and trust cannot be ordered up from the store. A person must remain in a post long enough for others to judge the consequences of his or her actions and decisions. One-year assignments will seldom cover the feedback loop. Even more important is the necessity to be ruthless if the confidence turns out to be unjustified. If you do not have confidence in a member of the team, that member must go. If the whole team does not merit confidence, the team must go. Without mutual confidence the principle of subsidiarity cannot work. Checks and checkers are necessary. Suspicion and evasion become rife, morale declines, the work deteriorates, and any remaining confidence evaporates. Mistakes can and should be tolerated, provided one learns from them, but too many mistakes erode confidence, particularly if they are what one company, W.L. Gore, calls "below-the-waterline" mistakes, mistakes that imperil the organization. Those are not easily forgiven. It is better to be tough than sorry.

Tom Peters tells an interesting story of Mike Walsh taking on the job of turning around Teneco. Four months into the job he heard that managers at the Louisiana site had called the employees together for a "safety meeting." When the workers arrived they were told to lie on the ground and were searched for drugs. This, felt Walsh, was not going to help the kind of organization he was trying to create. He flew to the site, apologized for the search, and used the occasion for another general meeting. During the meeting some employees started to complain about a safety problem in some of the bunk cars where the employees lived when on the site. Local managers started to explain away the problem by detailing how much the company spent on bunk car maintenance. Walsh interrupted. "Why not just visit the cars?" "But it's raining outside," some of the managers said. "It's OK," Walsh told them, "managers won't melt." He visited the bunk cars, decided that they were indeed unsafe, and saw to it that they were fixed.

That action may not have seemed very important in the great scheme of things at Teneco, but stories spread, and it helped greatly to establish the two-way confidence essential to subsidiarity. Confidence depends in the end on knowing who the other people are, what they stand for, how far they will go—on basic human qualities like authenticity, integrity, character. These are a far cry from the spreadsheets and committees that permeate organizational life. Tom Peters devotes a whole chapter in his book *Liberation Management* to "The Missing X-Factor: Trust," but has no easy solutions to offer. "Read more novels and fewer business books," he says. "Relationships really are all there is."

Subsidiarity sounds like another ugly word—empowerment. There is a significant difference. Empowerment implies that someone on high is giving away power. Subsidiarity, on the other hand, implies that the power properly belongs, in the first place, lower down or further out. You take it away as a last resort. Those in the center are the servants of the parts. The task of the center, and of any leader, is to help the individual or the group to live up to their responsibilities, to enable them to deserve their subsidiarity. In this way it is possible to handle one of the paradoxes of individualism, that we want to belong but we don't want to be bossed around, or to be "empowered" if the hidden message is "I empower you to do this, but I can disempower you if I don't like the way you do it." Subsidiarity is a tough deal, one has to understand one's responsibilities and then deliver. It means, too, that we have to face up to disagreements. If we are going to take responsibility, we need to be clear about what the criteria for our success are to be, what is acceptable and what is not. Only if there is mutual confidence can disagreement, argument, and conflict be handled positively. Organizations based on subsidiarity are full of ambiguity and argument and conflict, but if it is argument among trusted friends, united by a common purpose, then it is useful argument. Truth, said the Scottish philosopher David Hume, springs from arguments among friends.

It is extremely demanding to run an organization on the basis of reverse delegation and confidence. It also feels quite lonely at the center. As one director of ABB commented, "All we can do is to watch the herd and observe, with some relief, that in general it is heading in a westerly direction!" Why, then, are so many organizations trying to make it work? Partly in response to the paradox of individualism, the recognition that the well-educated knowledge worker increasingly wants both freedom and structure. To attract and keep the best of these knowledge workers, to be a so-called preferred organization, a firm has to guarantee subsidiarity.

Most of us are little different from the knowledge worker. We want to own our work, but we like to work within a structure. We need to know what is expected of us but have the discretion to do it our way. Subsidiarity is also, and more urgently, a response to the need in our institutions to be flexible but coherent, to be all things to all people but still recognizably the same to all. Deep down, however, subsidiarity is a moral imperative— power belongs to the people, it is the manager's, or teacher's, or parent's challenge to help them to exercise it responsibly.

Subsidiarity, with its emphasis on individual rights and duties, is the basis of any concept of citizenship and critical to any concept of society. If we want our personal freedoms, and if we want them underwritten with guarantees of health care and welfare, we must accept responsibility for our fellows and earn the confidence that will allow the freedoms. That is the kind of thing one learns from parents as much as from teachers, but, then, the messages implicit in subsidiarity are a good guide to parenthood. Give children as much responsibility as they can handle and help them live up to it. Subsidiarity is an old word, packed with meaning. It may sound out-of-date but it carries a modern punch. We would be foolish to discard it.

THE MEANING OF BUSINESS

● THE MEANING OF BUSINESS

A book that challenges us to find our human selves
again, amid all the pressures for progress and economic
success, must examine the place and meaning of business
in our societies. Even those who lead lives far removed
from the factories and shops of manufacturing and com-
merce need to have a view on the point of business,
whom and what it is for. Directly or indirectly, their economic well-being depends on it. A recession brings home
to everyone the importance of a healthy trading sector.
When business declines, everything is affected—jobs, tax
receipts, house prices, government spending. Does this
mean that business is purely a wealth-creating instrument, best left alone to do what it has to do, or does it
mean that, precisely because of its social impact, it has to
recognize a wider accountability than making its owners
seriously rich?

More directly, the business ethos has invaded most
of the rest of our life. Everything is now thought of as a
business of a sort. We are all "in business" these days, be
we a doctor or a priest, a professor or a volunteer. *Every*

organization is, in practice, a business, because it is judged by its effectiveness in turning inputs into outputs for its customers or clients, and is judged in competition against its peers. The only difference is that the "social businesses" do not distribute their surpluses. Americans, I was once assured, have always known this, but until lately the hard reality of it had escaped most Europeans.

Britain, however, has recently turned its schools, hospitals, and medical practices, and even the delivery parts of the government service, into independent businesses, still funded by the state but judged by their effective use of resources and required to compete for customers. When the full implications of what it means to be "business-like" sink in, we shall realize what a revolution it will be. One of the implications is that all these organizations, in which one-third of our people work, will all have to answer the same difficult questions: What is this business for? To whom does it belong? Are we who work in these businesses, be they social or commercial, something more than their instruments? What are our rights, and, conversely, our responsibilities?

The West has managed to evade most of these questions because we were preoccupied with our common enemy, communism. Anything, we assumed, must be better than such a centrally controlled system, conveniently ignoring the fact that many of our largest organizations were run in a similar way. Now that communism has been discredited, capitalism must be its own sternest critic. Anglo-Saxon capitalism, when exported in all its nakedness to the old socialist countries of Eastern Europe, is revealed to be good for some but not, obviously, for the many. It is, also, increasingly clear that there is more than one variant of capitalism. Michel Albert has spelled out the differences between the Anglo-Saxon version and the continental European version in his book, aptly called *Capitalism Against Capitalism*. But there is also the capitalism of Asia, what might be called Confucian capitalism, and, in particular, its Japanese variant.

The Anglo-Saxons have much to learn from the other varieties. Some people hoped that Britain and American businesses would start to emulate the way in which the Japanese and the continental Europeans developed a form of Chinese contract with their six stakeholders: financiers, employees, and suppliers most obviously, but also customers and the environment and society as a whole. Such a six-sided, or hexagon contract inevitably changes the priorities of the business, leaving more room for the concerns of the other parties. A business is no longer just an economic instrument. Ironically, the pressures of competing in a global world are pulling the others toward the Anglo-American model as fast as they move toward it.

The question "What is a business for?" is addressed in Chapter 8, in which I argue that the different systems of capitalism do indeed need to move together, borrowing the best of each other's traditions, in order to forge a new capitalism, one more obviously in the service of its society, but still flexible and efficient.

The other question, "To whom does a business belong?", is equally tendentious. I question whether the idea of a company as a piece of property which can be owned by anyone with enough money to pay for it, or bits of it, a property which can be bought and sold over the heads of those who work there, is still a valid concept in an age when people, not things, are a business's real assets. Property is certainly not a valid concept when we think of the new "social businesses." So what sort of institutions are they? Instead of arguing who the rightful owners ought to be, I suggest a third angle—that ownership is not a valid or relevant concept, any more than property is. We ought instead to think of "membership."

The consequences of this line of thought are explored in Chapter 9. Membership gives meaning, and responsibility, to those who work in the business. They cease to be instruments or employees and become enfranchised. Ironically, if we return to the old meaning of the "company," we realize that a company was a group of companions. That original meaning still lingers on in the occasional theatrical company, or in some of the old livery companies in London, now charities, not businesses. Perhaps we should rediscover the original meaning of the word.

The concept of a company in this sense already exists in the way many volunteer groups and not-for-profit organizations think of themselves. Just as these organizations are becoming more business-like, so we may see businesses looking to the nonprofit arena for new models. The nonprofit world understands all too well the combination of core funding and optional space, and the doughnut principle, and is familiar with the necessity of Chinese contracts in a good cause. These organizations may, unexpectedly, hold the clues to the second curve of capitalism.

There are more clues in places as far apart as Michigan and Brazil. We need many more if capitalism is to prove that it has a human face, that it is for the benefit of all and not a favored few, and that we do not have to lose ourselves in order to win.

8 *The Corporate Contract*

Capitalism has, supposedly, triumphed. There is demonstrably, some claim, no better way to run our societies than a mix of liberal democracy and free market enterprise. Business gives wealth and opportunity to us all. Consultants and economists from the West swarm into the new market economies of central Europe, with their overnight cases, to show them how to do it our way in 24 hours flat.

CAPITALISM

TRIUMPHANT?

The first results of the new capitalism are, however, far from reassuring. Industrial output in Poland fell by 35% between 1989 and 1991, inflation reached 260%. In

Hungary, arguably the best-prepared of the new economies for the transition, food and basic expenses absorbed 45% of the average household's expenses in 1989 but 70% in 1991. In the Czech Republic they hoped, at best, to keep the fall in real wages to 12% in 1991 and 10% in 1992. Russia is still a catastrophe, where the figures do not even make sense.

The full sad saga is forcefully described by William Keegan in his book *The Spectre of Capitalism*, where he comments:

> The terrible thing about the *sudden* adoption of capitalism is that the two necessary conditions preached by the reformers are in conflict. "Price Liberalisation," needed to make the markets work . . . almost inevitably involves a disturbing acceleration in inflation as people rush to protect themselves from higher prices. "Stabilisation" is, then, an uphill task in the face of "liberalisation."

The paradox is hard to balance. It was a director of West Germany's Audi who said, "There are lots of books on how to move from capitalism to socialism, but none on how to do it the other way round." He added, ruefully, "We seem to be doing the research for that new book!"

Western capitalism in countries like Russia has come to mean "trading." The black market and mafias abound. "Yellow-Page" services proliferate. Street bazaars and backyard markets are everywhere. Keegan reports that people can buy cars in Poland and, 48 hours later, sell them in Moscow for profits equivalent to ten years of a professor's salary. Visitors happily spend the annual salary of a Russian on a piece of fashion or a call girl. Such Wild East capitalism, he says, is never going to be the foundation of a proper market economy. Nor does it, at present, seem to promise the sort of freedom to shape our lives that many hoped for.

Big manufacturing enterprises are lacking, but a country as large as Russia cannot survive on services and trades alone, nor will it be content to be the cheap labor shop for Europe. "We used to build rockets to circumnavigate the moon in this plant," said one Russian colonel. "Are we to turn round and make pots and pans to compete with central Asia?" Even in Hungary, only 10% of the larger enterprises have been privatized. Most of the rest are probably not viable on their own.

Keegan was writing about Eastern Europe. My fear is that he could have been describing a possible scenario for Britain and America in a few years' time. The version of capitalism so triumphantly carried to those countries is the Anglo-American version. There are other versions, notably those of Japan and continental Europe, which have had a better record of combining liberalization and stability. They have done a better job of balancing economic freedom with relative equality, of giving more chances to more people.

The different versions of capitalism share certain fundamentals—free markets, the private ownership of assets, private direction of investment. They also share the idea of the hexagon contract. Where they differ is in the emphasis they give to each of the interest groups. The difference is highlighted by the answer each version would give to the question "What is a business for?"

WHAT IS
A BUSINESS FOR?

In my American business school in the sixties the answer was clear. It was inscribed above the blackboard in every class so that we could not ignore it—"maximize the medium-term earnings per share." Medium-term, mark you, not short-term, and maximize, not optimize. Twenty-five years later things had not changed. Just before announcing his resignation as Chief Executive of IBM, John Akers complained that "the average IBM'er has lost sight of the reasons for his company's existence. IBM exists to provide a return on invested capital to the stockholders."

From this basic premise all else flowed, given, of course, a perfect and intelligent market, managers who were clever, energetic, and wise, and an educational system that provided an intelligent and rational workforce. Looking back, it is amazing that none of us challenged either the premise or the assumptions. Yet my own life up to then should have given it the lie. I had been the lowly regional manager in a distant outpost of a great oil company. I suppose that I must have seen the published results of the company but its earnings per share, its profitability, did not keep me awake at night, nor make me leap out of bed in the morning. I was not a fool. I knew that any new project, rationally, needed to earn a rate of return above a certain figure, and mine were always expected to do just that, although neither I nor, as far as I know, anyone else ever checked whether those projects in fact lived up to their estimates.

If I'm honest, it was not the shareholders but my

own self-respect which drove me. Sitting in that far-off country, the idea of maximum earnings per share was very remote, very intellectual, very unreal. I had, I was sure, a much more serious social function, as I told a maiden greataunt back in Ireland who had complained that I was the first of the family to go into "trade." I was there to help produce things which were badly needed, in good condition, at a fair price, on time, without mucking up the local scenery or upsetting the local councillors or villagers among whom we lived and worked. It was a form of social contract, but, it needed profits to make it work and go on working.

My business school in America was wrong, I am now convinced. The principal purpose of a company is not to make a profit, full stop. It is to make a profit in order to continue to do things or make things, and to do so ever better and more abundantly. To say that profit is a means to other ends and not an end in itself is not a semantic quibble, it is a serious moral point. A requirement is not a purpose. In everyday life those who make the means into ends are usually called neurotic or obsessive. We have to eat to live, but if we live to eat we become distorted in more senses than one. In ethics, to mistake the means for the ends is to be turned in on oneself, one of the worst of sins, said Saint Augustine.

"Profits are the principal yardstick," stated the Watkinson Report on the responsibilities of the British public company 20 years ago, but a yardstick for what? And how can a yardstick be a purpose? It's like saying that you play cricket to get a good batting average. Wrong. You need a good average to keep on playing and to get into the first team. We need to clean up our logic.

DIFFERENT CULTURES,
DIFFERENT DREAMS

Lester Thurow, in his book *Head to Head,* argues that Anglo-Saxon economics stem from the Anglo-Saxon emphasis on the individual and, in particular, on the individual
as consumer. The individual is not as interested in the
work itself as in the results which that work will produce
for himself or herself. Personal wealth is the result the Anglo-Saxon wants, because that wealth will make possible
the life-style he envisions. The work is a means to an
end, not an end in itself.

Take, for instance, William Caxton, who brought
the printing press to England in 1477, an early example
of technological pioneering: "Caxton was an early and
prominent example of a well-known modern type," says
Anthony Glyn, "the individualistic Englishman following
out his own hobbies . . . . As a successful merchant he
made enough money during thirty years to devote his
later life to the literary pursuits he loved." British busi-
nessmen, when pressed for their real purpose in life,
nearly always say that they want to make their pile and
then do something "which really interests" them. Business is a means to an end. The end is money, and money
soon, but to use on something else.

The British businessman tends not to be interested
in sustained continuity. Private businesses, for instance,
seldom turn into third- or fourth-generation family businesses. They are sold or go public long before then.
Many a British entrepreneur would feel that asking the
next generation to take on the business would be to con-
strain its freedom. The Victorians who built Britain's in-

dustrial fortunes wanted their children to have nothing to do with business, but to be country gentlemen.

It is different in Japan. Thurow describes the Japanese business leaders as empire builders and social builders, gaining satisfaction from being part of a great and growing empire. To such people the use and ownership of production goods may be more important than consumption goods; they would, in fact, be happy to trade personal consumption for the success of "their" empire. Imperial Rome, he points out, had many more grand public buildings than fancy private homes. In America it is often the other way around.

Japanese workers join a firm in much the same way as volunteers join an army, not for personal wealth or glory, but to be part of a great endeavor. Today it is the business enterprise that offers the best chance for empire building. Given those attitudes, it is hardly surprising that the Japanese put long-term growth above short- or even medium-term profits. Indeed, profitability calculations hardly figure in some of their strategic decisions. To keep IBM at bay, Fujitsu won the computer contract for the water-distribution system of Hiroshima City with a bid of just one yen. The required rate of return for a ten-year R&D project averages 8.7% in Japan compared with 20.3% in the United States and 23.7% in the United Kingdom. As a result, there is naturally more investment in the future in Japan than in the other countries. In 1992, Japan invested the equivalent of 34.2% of its GDP in fixed assets. The figure was 16% in the United Kingdom and 14.8% in the United States.

Germany is different again. Germany thinks of itself as having a "social market" economy, not just a "market" economy. Business is seen as serving all the people, not just shareholders or even employees. Heinrich Henzler, the chairman of McKinsey's German offices, has written that: "Laws on co-determination, combined with a tradition of patriarchal concern, have made European C.E.O.s deeply committed to their employees, treating them more like partners in a long-term enterprise than anonymous 'factors of production.'" When he says European he means, I fear, continental Europe, not Britain. He goes on to argue that this is a source of great competitive advantage.

Every employer in Germany of any size regards it as part of its duty to take part in the "dual system" of workplace training, even though it may not employ the trainees at the end. They see that training as an investment in the continuity of German business, of which they will be a continuing part. The *Mittelstand,* the family businesses which are the backbone of the German economy, rarely sell out to others but are seen as a trust to be carried on by the family.

One reason for the small size of the German stockmarket (only 665 stocks are quoted compared with 2,300 in the smaller economy of the United Kingdom) is that the pension plans of these smaller firms are unfunded. The pension money is held in the company. The assumption is that the firms will always be around and be able to pay the pensions of their ex-workers. It also assumes that those workers would naturally want to work for the same company all their lives. Continuity is built into the system along with an acceptance of expensive social welfare policies, designed to take good care of those who are temporarily outside the system. German business exists for the good of all.

It helps, of course, that the firms are allowed tax relief on the reserves which they build up to pay those pensions, but they have the choice as to how they use those reserves, unlike the separately funded pension schemes of British and American firms where the monies are managed by outsiders, charged with considering only the interests of the pensioners. Not unnaturally, the German firms often use those reserve funds to re-inforce their links with key suppliers or agents by investing some of the reserves in their businesses, just as the Japanese do with *their* unfunded pension reserves. It is another force for continuity.

The role of the banks re-inforces the sense of continuity. The banks are not short-term financial helpers, concerned that their money is secure so that they can call it back to lend to others who are a better or more profitable risk. German banks are there for the long haul, with a stake in the business. In 1987, *The Economist* calculated that the large banks owned 10% to 25% of the shares in 48 of the 100 largest firms, 25% to 50% of the shares in 43 others, and over 50% of 9. In other words, every major firm was locked into the big bank network and vice versa. No wonder that contested takeovers are almost unknown in Germany. They would not succeed.

THE NEW
BLEND

Our versions of capitalism are the products of our histories. As a German foreign minister once said, "The British were very generous after the war, they insisted on federalism, co-determination and single plant unions for us but took none of these for themselves!" Thurow and Keegan are not alone in seeing problems with the Anglo-American version, with its hint of selfishness, and favoring the German model, accepting that the Japanese version is probably unique to their culture. The Chinese, for instance, with a history of family enterprises, are closer to the Italians and the Germans than to their Japanese neighbors.

Paradoxically, however, although the German and Japanese models have been clearly the most successful in building rich and relatively equal societies, there are signs that as the world becomes one marketplace, the versatility of the Western-style capital markets and the freedom of the individual in the Anglo-Saxon cultures become seductive. The third generation of the mittelstand families are not as keen as their forebears on the idea of a family trust if it locks them into one firm and one town for life. Pensions will soon be funded and that money will boost the German stockmarket—to thrice its size in ten years, some think. Meantime as both the Germans and the Japanese acquire foreign shareholders in their pursuit of global empires, they are meeting with investors who cannot be expected to share the Japanese quest for economic supremacy, but want shorter-term rewards.

As a result, the balance of forces among the six interest groups is changing in all the countries. In Anglo-Saxon capitalism the shareholders have, traditionally, come first, with the other parties seen as a constraint, legitimate perhaps, but still a constraint. It is now accepted that all the so-called stakeholders matter. The principle of the hexagon contract is now written into most corporate statements of purpose, even if the shareholder is still the first. The shareholder has to be the core of the corporate doughnut, but it is widely agreed that the business is not fully developed unless the interests of the other stakeholders fill the empty space in the doughnut. A business has to have a "license to operate" from its surrounding stakeholders.

In Silicon Valley a new form of *keiretsu* is emerging to rival the Japanese variety, a network of interlocking groups who have more to gain from the continued growth of the business than from its immediate profitability. These include venture capital companies, lawyers, accountants, scientists, investors, real estate firms, trained managers, and equipment suppliers. Together, they form a network of influence, balancing the forces affecting the company.

In Japan the usual view is that the employees come at the top of the list, but Akio Morita of Sony maintains that it is really the customer who comes first, not from any idealistic notion of wanting to please the man or woman in the street, but because the customer represents the empire they are seeking to build. Morita is now sounding cautious, because he senses a backlash from competitor countries that resent the competitive advantage Japanese companies obtain by starving the other stakeholders in order to keep prices low for the customer. A re-adjustment is needed, partly for the sake of global harmony but partly to placate the other stakeholders who would like bigger pickings.

In Germany there has always been a very conscious effort to balance the interests of the six stakeholders. Henzler calls it "a social balancing act," arguing that business in his country has always accepted that homelessness, illiteracy, and other social ills are not only morally unacceptable but also economically harmful. Business has therefore been willing to bear the considerable social overhead because of its long-term benefits. Some rebalancing is now starting.

In the past, German firms refused to trade their stock on the New York Stock Exchange, arguing that the requirement to publish quarterly reports distorted the priorities of the business and distracted management from its proper longer-term concerns. Recently, the need for funds to finance its restructuring and expansion has forced Daimler-Benz to change its mind. Others will follow. Foreign stockholders will not share the preoccupation with Germany's social balancing act, any more than they want to encourage Japan's economic empire building. German investors, too, want more than they have been getting. A recent survey of 11 stockmarkets over the past 20 years ranked Germany ninth in terms of returns to investors. These investors are now growing restive. One group is even suing Deutsche Bank.

Even without outside pressure, German business is worried lest the cost of the social balancing act may have grown too high. Jobs are draining out of Germany. BMW sites its new factory in America, Volkswagen is looking to Spain for its mega-plant. Hungary and the Czech Republic are close neighbors with skilled labor at a quarter the cost of German labor, even in the east of the country. The social costs of that eastern part are also stretching consensus to a breaking point. One young German executive put it dramatically: "If they had to buy some underdeveloped country," she said, bitterly, "why couldn't they have chosen a smaller cheaper one?" The new generation of Germans may not be as prepared to pay the price for social cohesion as their parents were.

THE EXISTENTIAL COMPANY

As the cultures blend, the purposes of a business become less clear. Germany's social balancing act, Japan's economic imperialism, America's and Britain's priority on returns to owners, all become more muted as the other forces in the hexagon contract become more powerful. What then is a company for in this more blended world? The only real answer, I suggest, is "for itself." We might call it the existential company.

The existential company operates with the hexagon contract, but within the bounds of that contract it is primarily concerned with growth and development. Its continued existence, its immortality, is its purpose. It may turn out not to deserve immortality—the life cycle of the average public company is only 40 years—but it is a worthy goal because unless all six interest groups are satisfied, the company will be unlikely to live that long. I liked the family business head who said, looking down at the roofs of the little Belgian town which was dominated, and employed, by his firm, "We had to sit out two world wars, but they counted on us. In a family business you have to think beyond the grave."

No one can lay claim to immortality. It has to be deserved. A company will only be allowed to survive as long as it is doing something useful, at a cost that people can afford, and that generates enough funds for its continued growth and development. Existentialism in business is not a form of selfishness. There has to be what James O'Toole, in America, has called "stakeholder symmetry," and most of those stakeholders are likely to have a vested interest in immortality. Employees, customers, suppliers, and the community would prefer that a business continue, as long as it is good. Even shareholders, now that so many of the institutions are locked into their stakes because they are too large to switch around, will settle for "continuity provided it is justified by the results."

Stakeholder symmetry doesn't get the blood beating any faster than shareholder value, which is why I prefer to settle for immortality.

BETTER, NOT BIGGER

What, then, would be the purpose of such an existential company? The answer will be different for every business. Satisfying its financiers is a necessary condition, the core of the business doughnut, as is satisfying its customers and the other stakeholders, but a necessary condition is not a purpose. That purpose may be, as in Japan, to conquer the world, but it can be less grandiose. You can grow without wanting to be the biggest or even big.

After one sun-drenched day in the wine country of Northern California I asked the owner of the winery about the future. He was passionate about his winery, he said; he was putting back every cent he could into its growth. "Where can you grow?" I asked, looking around at the valley where every inch of land was by now fully planted with other people's vines. "Oh, I don't want to expand," he said. "I want to grow better not bigger."

Better, not bigger. It is one definition of a purpose, one way to grow, one recipe for immortality. What we *are* can be as important an aspect of purpose as what we *do*. The existential hexagon company would require some changes in the law, at least in Britain and America, because the rights of the shareholders would be severely curtailed. Perhaps not. The law in both countries already recognizes the company as an entity in its own right. Lord Justice Evershed, summing up in 1947, said, "Shareholders are not, in the eyes of the law, part owners of the undertaking. The undertaking is something different from the totality of its shareholdings."

The judge was describing an existential company, one that exists in its own right, something with a life and a future of its own. He was suggesting that all companies are, in law, existential. We have to take that judgment seriously, and give it meaning. We have to assume that every company has a life of its own which needs purpose and direction. It is an end in itself, not an instrument owned by others. If we don't, if there is no shared sense of identity to which all parties subscribe, there will be little chance of finding a compromise between the interests of different groups. Each will, then, quite understandably fight their corner and the toughest requirement will become the dominant purpose.

TO FIND
A PURPOSE

The Anglo-Saxon countries do not start with the cultural beliefs of Japan and Germany. Business leaders will have to create that purpose which commands assent. Essential though profitability is for the continued existence and growth of a business, it begs the questions "For whom?" and "For what?"; it is not, in itself, enough. At present, to many people the answer to those questions seems to be "the shareholders" and "their enrichment." The managers, with a proportion of their rewards linked to the share price, are seen as being allied to the shareholders rather than to the workers, unlike those of other countries. The workers and the other stakeholders in the hexagon are seen by the managers as costs, and costs are things which, instinctively, we seek to reduce. There is seldom a shared sense of belonging.

In one week in the recession-afflicted Britain of 1993, four large public companies reported huge drops in profits, turning them into loss makers in two instances, but did not lower their dividends. As the president of Britain's Board of Trade commented at the time, "Presumably the implication is that shareholders can make more money by withdrawing their funds from the business than by allowing the business to invest in itself." It does not say much for the hope of immortality in those companies.

Again, the figures speak for themselves: since 1975, British companies have retained, on average, 45% of their profits for re-investment, American firms 54%, Japanese firms 63%, and German firms 67%. In such a situation it made perfect sense, as it still does, for British shareholders to take their money out of generous British firms and invest it overseas where the companies clearly believe in their own long-term future.

Not all Anglo-Saxon companies think that way. Johnson & Johnson's credo is famous in America. Formulated four decades ago by President Robert Wood Johnson, it lists corporate priorities:

- service to its customers comes first

- service to its employees and management comes second

- service to the community comes third

- service to its stockholders comes last.

The credo was put to the test during the Tylenol affair when some bottles of its best-selling Tylenol were tampered with, and several people died. J&J responded by pulling all 30 million capsules off the shelves. In the long term it gained because its reputation soared.

Johnson & Johnson might not be so renowned for its credo in America if it wasn't so unusual. It is no different from the batting order in any Japanese company. In a study by Fons Trompenaars, managers from different countries were asked if they agreed with the statement that the bottom line should be the only real goal of a business, or if the other stakeholders should be taken into account. Ninety-six percent of Japanese managers agreed as did 86% of the Germans, but only 53% of Americans. The British were in between at 78% in favor of the stakeholder balance.

If we don't change our ways more quickly, capitalism in our lands may deteriorate into the kind of Wild East now seen in central Europe, although at a higher level of consumption and corruption no doubt. To think in terms of an existential company, striving for growth and immortality within the hexagon is one handle on the problem. Another is to re-think what we mean by a "company."

9 *The Membership Business*

A business is owned by its shareholders. It is, when you stop to think about it, a strange type of ownership. To begin with, those owners normally have limited liability, something that goes with no other form of ownership that I can think of. Second, the "thing" they own consists mostly of people. Owning people, no matter how well you treat them, is considered wrong in every other part of life. There was once a time, in parts of Europe, where a man, by law, owned his wife. No one now, however anti-feminist, would think that right.

The reasons are to be found in history, but history, I have argued before, is not necessarily the best guide to the future. Limited liability was a most ingenious invention which allowed private businesses to take the risks which expansion required. It was a privilege given a century and a half ago, to people who really did own their businesses, ran them, and stood or fell by their success. They were locked into the fortunes of their enterprises. The "property" they owned was bricks and mortar, machines, and raw materials. The people were "hands," employed to work the property, just as they used to be employed to work the land. It made sense, if they were to expand as fast as they might, that they should not have to put all their personal wealth at stake. Hence the privilege, granted to the people of a certain time and of a certain tradition. With the privilege came some implied responsibilities for the welfare of the workers and the quality of the work. These responsibilities were not always honored, but the privilege of ownership and limited liability endured. Without it the railways of Britain, for instance, would never have been built, nor would the Industrial revolution have happened on the scale it did. Whether what was right then is right now is another question.

OWNERS OR PUNTERS?

Ownership may no longer be the appropriate concept, but if it is, it is the proprietors of the private businesses who have the best claim to be the inheritors of that tradition. Their futures are tied to the futures of the business. For publicly owned businesses the situation is different. The "owners" of these companies are, for the most part, institutions—investment funds, pension funds, insurance companies. They have no direct involvement with the business. They do not manage it or work in it. They do not know those who do. They are not locked in. Average shareholding by the big institutional investors in Britain is four years. Their responsibility is discardable. If things are not going well, their best strategy is to sell their shares. Fair enough. The rules allow it and their own shareholders or fundholders require it. The result is to turn the shareholders of public companies into what *The Economist* once called "punters," equating them with the backers of racehorses at the track.

To expect the punters who backed the bay gelding to stay with that horse throughout its career, or to insist that the trainer take their advice, is not reasonable. If they don't like its form, they transfer their money to another nag. Punters or speculators they may be, owners in any real sense they cannot be. Devices to lock them in by tax incentives or legal requirements would be but "sand in a free market," as these devices were once described. Nevertheless punters have an extraordinary privilege. They are, for the price of their bets, given a vote from time to time in the auction ring as to who should own their horse. This means that they have to be wooed, continually, for who knows when the bell for the auction may toll? Under these rules every public company is potentially up for sale every day.

It is argued that the constant possibility of the auction ring concentrates the mind of the trainer. It has been known to do that for the occasional bad trainer. It certainly concentrates his or her attention on the price and away from the good of the animal. The two are not necessarily the same thing. I asked one supermarket chairman why he was expanding so energetically into France and Belgium, buying up competitors wherever possible. Was it to take advantage of the enlarged European market? "No," he replied, "we want to make ourselves so big and so complicated that no one will be

tempted to swallow us up." The best defense against being bought in that ring is, apparently, to buy. Yet all the
evidence is that the bidder does worse, most times, than
the loser at the end of the day. The cost is, presumably,
justified if it gives one protection from the diversion of
the auction ring, but it does nothing for the original
business.

Some say that making the managers, and perhaps
the workers, into the owners removes the pressures of the
auction ring. But the history of management buyouts in
recent years suggests that owner-managers are just as sus-
ceptible to large offers as anyone else. I have known quite
a few who profess a dedication to long-term stewardship
in October, only to be out to pasture, richer by several
millions, in November.

Others look to the creation of a consortium of institutions that will act as proper long-term owners—banks,
pension funds, mutual funds, and other companies—leaving other punters to flutter in the margin without affecting
the long-term ownership. The pension funds that own
more than half of all British or American shares are responsible for other people's money and have always
shied away from locking themselves in. In America they
are not even allowed to sit on the boards of the companies in which they invest.

Some hope that the size of the funds involved will
effectively lock the institutions into the index of stocks so
that they will be content to stay where they are. There is
little sign that those institutions, or, more precisely, their
fund managers, will be content to be so inactive as punters. And as for individual shareholders, one report predicted that the last individual shareholding in Wall Street
would be sold in 2003. The idea that we could become a

nation of small independent shareholders, which some dream of, is just that, a dream. Whether they would, in any case, behave any differently from their bigger brethren is open to doubt. Why should they?

There are a few signs that the punters are being pushed into behaving more like real owners. Some state legislation in the United States has made hostile takeovers more difficult, forcing the shareholders to put pressure on the boards of corporations if they want change instead of waiting for someone else to buy them out. Several chairmen of major companies in the United States and Britain have "retired" rather more precipitately than they expected to as a result of this pressure, but usually too late and leaving too much for their successor to do.

PROPERTY OR COMMUNITY?

Instead of fiddling with the rules, we ought to ask whether we are still playing the same game. Why is it sensible to think of an organized group of people as a piece of property, to be bought and sold according to its market price? Because that is what companies really are these days, organizations of people. A business does not have to be as rarefied as Microsoft to realize that its key assets are its human resources and the kinds of intellectual advantage that they carry around with them—not just their creativity and technical knowledge, but also their networks of contacts, their human skills, and their experience. Everyone accepts that Japan's economic success has nothing to do with raw materials but is entirely based on the way it educates and manages people. We have been slow to draw the obvious conclusion, that the same might have to be true for the rest of us. We must make our people our assets, and turn most of our property into the intellectual variety.

"Intellectual property" is a neat phrase, but it may delude us into thinking that the same traditions of ownership can continue. They can't. Intellectual property means people. Organizations are nothing if they are not communities of people, and a community is not a property. A community is not a commodity to be bought or sold. A community has "members," not "employees," and it belongs to its members—only outsiders, not insiders, get to be "employed" or hired by the community. If it needs money, it raises loans or mortgages, secured, perhaps, against part of the physical assets. It could, conceivably, sell a share in the future stream of net income—a form of equity—so that its financiers could share in its fortunes, but such a share would give no other rights. A community belongs to its members.

What would this mean in practice? Businesses would be self-governing communities. Limited liability would still apply, justified once again because the business "belongs" only to its members. Financiers would, in effect, hold mortgages but could only intervene managerially if the business reneged on its payments. Some mortgages would carry no repayment obligation but, instead, receive a share of the income stream for perpetuity.

Mortgages could be traded, stockmarkets would continue but only as betting rings, not auction rings. Businesses would only merge or fold by decision of their members, who would probably take their financiers into their confidence. Outwardly, little would look different, but inside it would feel very different.

THE VIEW
FROM ABROAD

For slightly different reasons, in Japan and Germany the idea of the company as a community, and of financiers as mortgage holders, has long existed. Michel Albert calls it the Rhine model because it prevails in those countries that line the Rhine, but versions of it are found in Sweden and, with a slightly different twist, in Japan. It is, says Albert, who has worked with both the Rhine model of capitalism and the Anglo-Saxon variety, markedly different from the property concept of a company.

In Japan the shareholders are more like preference debenture holders; their dividends are related to the par value of the shares and not to the market value; many of them are suppliers or associates of the business and obtain rewards from doing business with a sound and growing company. They are the bankers, leasing companies, insurers, parts suppliers, distributors, and agents who, as Carl Kester points out in a recent study, see shareholding as the entry fee to a mutually beneficial system.

Unlike in the Anglo-Saxon tradition, the board and management in Japan are not representatives of the financiers but of the workers. Senior managers are not rewarded with share options, as in Britain and America. They are linked, through a bonus system, to the performance of their workforce, the other members of the company. By law, any merger or takeover requires the agreement of a majority of the directors of the company, but the directors are almost all insiders, career managers, representing the people with whom they work. If the financial returns are satisfactory the Japanese shareholder has almost no power.

Japanese companies will borrow fiercely to finance growth, but once secure, will do their best to finance future growth out of retained earnings. In the 1980s, Japanese companies, on average, carried four times as much debt as American companies. Toyota, an exception, had no debt at all and was known as the Bank of Toyota because of its self-contained financial strength. Toyota does not want its investors to be its controllers.

The much discussed lifetime employment policies of Japanese business also fit the community concept. Members of a community cannot be expelled. They are there for life. The Japanese company will, however, make sure that they have as few people in their organizing core as possible and that they are the best around. It is not always realized that the lifetime system applies only to men, only to large organizations, and only to full-time employees. It is generally thought that these true community members amount to less than 30% of the total workforce. No wonder there is such competition to join one of those business communities. No wonder, too, that the organizations spend so much time on the training and development of their people. They have no other choice. They can't sell their people assets and buy others.

In Germany and some of the other continental European countries the same concepts apply but for different historical reasons. Unlike Japanese, German business is not dominated by the big names. In 1989 *Business Week* listed the 1,000 biggest businesses in the world. There were 353 American firms, 345 Japanese, and 30 in Germany. Germany's strength, as noted, lies in its mittelstand, its small to medium-sized family businesses.

Tom Peters, who first revealed the mittelstand phenomenon to America, says that there are, maybe, 300,000 of these firms with from 10 to 3,000 employees. Less well known, but equally important, are the family businesses of Northern Italy making knitwear, textiles, bricks, tiles, furniture, hydraulics, farm machinery—the middle technology, design conscious products which are the staple ingredients of Italy's exports. The big industrial combines in Italy are mostly state owned.

These German and Italian businesses are families. They want global reach but not global size. They concentrate on what they know that they can do well and make sure that it is good enough to be among the best in the world. That way they can grow better without growing bigger and remain a family. Their financiers are investors rather than owners or controllers. They are the banks and insurance companies who are effectively locked in for the long term. They would find it difficult to get rid of their shares except to another friend of the business.

The point of these businesses is to be able to go on doing their work, profitably and enjoyably, for as long as possible. It is a way of life, not a means to an end. Since immortality is the point, and since shareholders are locked in and cannot be too greedy, the family heads inevitably think long term, invest enormous sums in innovation, and keep their core group small but excellent.

These businesses, however, are families, not communities which belong to the members. The head of the family is still the owner. The best of them, and not all of them are best or even good, think of themselves as responsible for not only their children's futures but the futures of their workers' children. That way it makes sense to trade off the short term for the longer opportunities. Tom Peters records that the mittelstand chiefs he met talked in terms of decades, not quarters, when, that is, they bothered to mention a time limit at all.

Family businesses, however, depend on the family for immortality, and that tends to be a fragile base. The Italians talk of the third-generation syndrome, when the family talent peters out or goes in search of other pastures; rags to riches and back again, as the British put it. Many of the mittelstand businesses are now approaching that third generation. The sigmoid curve is beginning to turn down for some. They are losing their innovative thrust, the family is becoming lazy, or greedy, or both. Some are looking for ways to sell. Immortality for the mittelstand would be better ensured if the family came to mean the family of workers. In the bigger companies the German concept of co-determination, which puts equal numbers of shareholders and workers on the supervisory board, is an attempt to create that sense of one family even in a large enterprise.

I suggested, in discussing the corporate contract, that companies could only keep the interest groups in balance if they were existential in the sense that they felt completely responsible for their own destiny. This is only possible if they are independent. To the Japanese the company is a community, to the continental Europeans the best companies are run like families. Neither concept appeals to the British or the Americans. Both sound weasly, undynamic. There is, however, an old Anglo-Saxon word with all the right history, until recently; it is "company," meaning a fellowship, a group of companions. Somewhere along the line it acquired its technical legal definition and lost its wider connotations. There was a time when we had the concept right.

THE RE-INVENTED "COMPANY"

The models of this old-style company already exist in our societies in some unlikely places. We can borrow their ways but not, I think, their names. There is, for instance, the club. A club is a place which belongs to its members and whose underlying purpose is its continued successful existence. It can best ensure that continuity by doing what it is best at doing. Its financiers are investors in its future, not owners or controllers, and its management works for the members, not the financiers.

Perhaps the most interesting models are to be found in the charitable and nonprofit worlds. These organizations are owned by no one. They have constitutions, members, boards of trustees as well as boards of management, sources of finance rather than shareholders, and their purpose is their meaning. They are not properties, they cannot be bought or sold, although they can join forces, merge, and make alliances. They have, in their doughnut, a core of professionals and, beyond it, a space full of helpers. These latter are often called "associates," with limited rights of membership. The title these organizations often have is that of "society." There is, in Britain, for example, a host of Royal Societies for this and that, all prestigious, all communities. *Société* is the word in France for a business, and it might also serve in the Anglo-Saxon countries, but it would be preferable to reinvent the company in its old meaning. The company would have a core of companions with associates in the space around the core. It would be existential, responsible for its own destiny within the constraints of its hexagon, striving for immortality by doing better what it does best.

THE SEPARATION
OF POWERS

Some will say a self-governing business is a license for abuse. Self-determination has been a charter for scoundrels down the ages. Not all businesses deserve immortality. True, but the market is a great corrective. Over time it sorts out the rotten apples in the system. That is not enough. Democracies, and federal democracies in particular, lay great store in the separation of powers. So it should be in the re-invented company.

The legislative, or policy-making, function is separate from the executive, or management, and from the judicial, or monitoring roles. The roles overlap—the executive will propose most of the policies, while the laws which the judicial branch enforces are laid down by the legislature, but the functions are distinct and usually performed by different people in different bodies. That practice is gradually being extended to organizations. It is seen most clearly in the charitable or nonprofit bodies where the board or council is quite separate from the executive and where, in Britain, there is an outside regulatory body, The Charity Commissioners, whose job is to ensure that the charity is doing what it said it would. Continental European countries also favor two-tier boards for their corporations.

Britain and America are going the same way although they typically give the management board the title of "Executive Committee." The Cadbury Report in Britain in 1992, on the financial requirements of corporate governance, recommended that the roles of chairman and chief executive be split, and that there should be a substantial group of outside directors on the board. That is a small step in the same direction. More corporations are also putting their judicial function under a separate hat, with board committees to ensure compliance with their own rules and standards. There is even talk of a small trustee board of independent shareholders with limited powers of inspection and oversight, for the accounts and the appointment of board members.

After a fracas with Virgin Airlines in 1993, British Airways set up a new committee of its board on compliance. Some said it was a case of shutting the stable door after the horse had bolted, but it was, nevertheless, another step toward a proper balance in what is, in effect, a self-governing body. In Volkswagen in Germany and Phar Mor in America large-scale fraud was apparently conducted for years without the board being aware of it.

Effective and independent control systems are critical to the governance of self-governing bodies. The powers need to be even more visibly separated and separately staffed in an existential company. It may be necessary to put the judicial or auditing powers in the hands of an independent regulator. This already happens where the industry is dominated by a small number of companies that are, thereby, largely in control of their own destiny.

One existential community which, for many years, would have no truck with the separation of powers, believing instead that a concentration of the three functions of policy, execution, and regulation would make it more effective, was Lloyd's of London, the insurance cooperative. They have changed things now, separating out the three roles into different bodies, but not before there had been a catalogue of frauds, mismanagement, and bad policies, resulting in losses to its "names," the members of this community, of some £5 billion over three years. There is a strong consensus that the concentration of powers led to a blindness to irregularities, to stupidity in strategy, and to laxity in management, rather than to increased effectiveness.

THE MEMBERSHIP CONTRACT

In the end, however, a self-governing club in a competitive system should only survive as long as it deserves to survive. One threat to that survival will be a constantly changing membership. There will be no pressure to plan for the future of the children if the fathers and mothers of those children are unlikely to be around in five years' time. The current tendency, in Britain and America, to use the organization as a stepping stone in a personal walk to glory and riches will make nonsense of an immortal club. Loyalty has to be reciprocal. Temporary contracts will beget temporary time horizons.

We need to see more lifetime contracts again, remembering that a corporate lifetime is going to be much shorter in the future. I can see a period of apprenticeship, or articles, for new, young employees, of perhaps five to seven years, followed by a fixed-term tenure contract of from ten to twenty years, during which time they will be full members of the company or club. Professor Iwao has calculated that the average stay by core staff in one firm in Japan is 14 years. Lifetime in practice means only long term. People might well serve their articles with one company and then join another as member, as accountants already do. After their membership period expires it could be renewed, or they may well "go portfolio," becoming independent advisers or suppliers to their old club. Membership will then be a privilege, akin to partnership but with limited liability, for a select minority—the core—requiring reciprocal obligations and loyalty.

In 1993 the director general of the BBC was discovered to have sold his services to the BBC through his own private company. This was a perfectly legal device in commercial television from which he had come. It was not thought appropriate in the culture of the BBC where long-term loyalty was the norm, even though it operates in the same industry. The feeling expressed by many was that this kind of loyalty could hardly be demanded from others if the head of the organization appeared to see his own job as a temporary assignment.

It was a dispute symbolic of the times. More and more professionals think of themselves as on a temporary assignment with an organization. Loyalty goes first to one's team or project, then to one's profession or discipline, and last to the organization where these skills are practiced. In the city, whole teams of dealers or analysts move together from one organization to another. Senior jobs in business are often on three-year contracts. Executives, like doctors, move from location to location as they advance their professional careers. Company loyalty will be very short term if this trend continues. The BBC was right to be alarmed.

My own belief, and hope, is that this trend, too, will be subject to the sigmoid curve and that companies will want to hug their key members to themselves for the duration of their shorter working lives. To do that they will need to give them all the benefits of membership, including the effective rights of ownership. These rights will have to go beyond the current fashion for share options, which gives them only a minority stake in the punters' bets, but will be something more akin to partnership, locking them in to a self-governing membership group. Only then will we find the motivation to plan for immortality. Few would want to commit themselves to an organization owned by punters.

If the business as a self-governing, membership organization is such a good idea, why don't we see more of them? The number, and the record, of cooperatives and their ilk is small, and, with some notable exceptions, poor. Cooperatives often confuse ownership and management. Because ownership is in common they also think that management has to be shared. Democracy, however, does not require that all who vote should also have the right to manage, or even to demand a referendum on every decision. That way chaos lies. The German and Japanese organizations do not make that mistake.

There are also the ESOP companies, the employee share ownership schemes that many companies have adopted as a way of giving their workers a stake in the organization. The evidence on these is mixed. Some make a difference to motivation and commitment, most don't seem to matter much either way. A well-researched study in America by Corey, Rosen, and others, found that the ones that did work had large employee contributions (8% to 10%), a true philosophy of partnership, and multiple ways of participating. The percentage of stock owned by employees made little difference, nor did the stockmarket performance of the shares. In other words, it was membership, not ownership, that really mattered. If there was no sense of membership, ownership made no difference.

In Britain, the best-known membership business is the John Lewis Partnership, with its chain of retail stores. This business belongs to its members, who receive dividends from its profits, elect a chairman, but entrust the management to a conventional executive structure. They do not, however, own shares they can sell. It is a true business community. It has had, however, few imitators.

This must be because we are hung up on the idea of property. It is largely the fault of an outmoded legal system, in Britain at least. George Goyder, in his book *The Just Enterprise,* points to a prescient comment by Lord Eustace Percy in 1944:

> Here is the most urgent challenge to political invention ever offered to the jurist and the statesman. The human association which in fact produces and distributes wealth, the association of workmen, managers, technicians and directors, is not an association recognized by the law. The association which the law does recognize—the association of shareholders, creditors and directors—is incapable of production or distribution and is not expected by the law to perform these functions. We have to give law to the real association and to withdraw meaningless privilege from the imaginary one.

Our rules do not allow for a wealth-creating club that is not someone's piece of property. It does make it difficult to balance the contradictions inherent in a company owned by some and worked by others, but managed by the agents of the owners because, whatever the rhetoric, it will be hard to find the elusive common purpose. Ultimately, we shall have to change the rules.

I take heart, however, from that research on share ownership plans. Ownership makes little difference unless there is a sense of membership. Therefore, presumably, the technical conditions of ownership make little difference if there is a real sense of membership. Laws tend to follow practice, not lead it. If we can create that sense of membership in our organizations, by more subsidiarity, more twin citizenship, more sharing of the added-value, closer teams and better boards, conceivably the so-called owners, would revert to their proper role, as financiers and owners only of last resort. The formal position would be irrelevant, as it is in Japan and, to a lesser extent, in Germany.

It is hard to conceive of our giant multinationals and other mass organizations becoming membership companies. We may, however, see these organizations breaking down into alliances of much smaller ones. You no longer have to be big to be global in the information age. *The Economist* has 55 journalists in London but covers the world, in scope and in readership. *The Economist,* too, is owned, in effect, by one proprietor who holds the bulk of the voting shares. Other financiers have stakes with smaller voting rights. There is a board of management to oversee the business, and a board of trustees to protect editorial freedom. Given its current benevolent proprietor, *The Economist* is almost a membership company. It feels like one when you visit it. Give voting shares to members and the model for the company would be complete.

Words and titles can help, even without the legal backing. It was when Ricardo Semler called his Directors "Counsellors," the Senior Managers "Partners," and everyone else "Associates," that he had to live up to the expectations the new words raised. If it worked as well as it did in the difficult conditions of the Brazilian economy, and without any change to the legal situation of ownership, it must be possible elsewhere. Ralph Sayer did the same at Johnsonville Foods, calling his workers "mem-

bers" and his managers "coordinators" in order to sym-
bolize the new order, one in which profit sharing and autonomy went hand-in-hand. We need not wait for the
law to change.

Membership is a way of thinking about the psychological contract between an individual and the organization. If the individual is seen as an instrument, even an
"empowered" instrument, he or she is there to be used
by others for their purposes. Such an instrumental contract, no matter how well intentioned or how benevo-
lently interpreted, is a denial of democracy. Our economic well-being and the continued success of capitalism
depend on efficient and effective organizations of all types.
One way, perhaps the only way, to match our needs for
democracy in our critical institutions with our need for
efficiency is to think of our organizations as membership
businesses.

A STATE OF JUSTICE

A State of Justice

The specter of a divided society looms over us, no matter how federated we are or how well-meaning our businesses. We have to tackle the paradox of justice and, in particular, the paradox of intelligence. If we don't, we may well bring the whole edifice down about our ears, because it is ultimately not tolerable for the many poor to live beside the few rich. In any event it would be crazy, as well as immoral, not to want to create a full property-owning democracy when intelligence is the property because of the happy paradox that more intelligence for some does not mean less for anyone else.

These chapters are not intended to be a discourse on the nature of justice. Justice is, however, the bond of society. Justice allows us to dwell together in unity, building a beneficial compromise between the rights of the individual and our responsibilities to our fellow human beings, enabling us to love both ourselves and our neighbors. If we want to avoid the specter of a divided and embattled society, we should do our best to create a state of justice in our land.

At its simplest, justice means fairness. Fairness means, for instance, that society should not deal with people arbitrarily but with "due process"—this is the legal side of justice. Fairness also means that not everyone should get the same, because not everyone needs or deserves the same. In practice strict equality does not work. As Abraham Lincoln said, you don't make the poor rich by making the rich poor. Fairness could mean, however, either that we gave the brightest of our young the best of our education because they would make the most of it, or that we gave the least talented the best because they needed it most. Fairness is always complicated.

Fairness, when it descends from lofty principles to hard decisions, means a compromise, a blend of two "oughts." In the case of education, for instance, fairness means that everyone should, as far as is practically possible, have the same chance to be different. We should not tilt the scales against anyone from the start. We should also give people more than one start if they are slow off the mark. On the other hand, we should also encourage those who make the most of that early start. No one should want to cut back on the education of doctors to create more schools for delinquents on the grounds that the latter need it more. Justice seeks to balance the needs of the individual with the needs of the wider community.

In the context of the issues discussed in this book, fairness means giving everyone a decent chance of a life on the second curve. In Britain, the Commission for Social Justice put it this way in their first report in 1993: "We cannot help but regard a commitment to the extent of opportunities as a radical doctrine, and one that lies at the heart of social justice." In a democracy where wealth derives from property, fairness, therefore, means giving everyone a chance to get some of that property, which, in the new millennium, means intelligence of one sort or another. Fairness therefore requires an investment in intelligence, an investment in the education of all people throughout their lives, realizing that some people will make more of that investment than others. Chapter 10 investigates what that might mean—the different types of intelligence, the forms education might take, and the help people might need to develop their skills and aptitudes. In a state of justice, everyone has a right to some property. What use they make of it, however, is up to them.

Fairness also suggests that there should be more chances to win in life than to lose. Another angle on this problem is to propose that there should be more than one measure of success. Where there is only one scale, there will always be winners and losers, and usually more losers than winners. In a contented society, with more winners than losers, there need to be multiple scales, a variety of ways to feel good and to count yourself successful. Society will then have more givers than takers, and a greater variety of life.

Chapter 11 looks at some of the alternatives to money as the measure of all things, and proposes a new scoreboard. What is counted is what counts. It is not enough, therefore, to say that a good life is more than jewels, or that the environment is important to all of us. We have to make a stab at measuring such good intentions or that is all that they will be, good intentions.

More measures will mean more compromises between the numbers on the scales, in personal life as well as in business and in society as a whole. The principle of the doughnut provides one path to that compromise. There is, however, no one answer for everyone. Justice requires that we eliminate the worst inequalities wherever we can. Justice does not require that all should be the same. That, in fact, would be unjust, a denial of our right to be different within limits.

10 The Intelligence Investment

WHEN INTELLIGENCE
IS PROPERTY

In a property-owning democracy which claims to be fair
to all its citizens, it is only right that everyone should
have a share in that property and the wealth it brings.
When property meant land, social and political revolutions redistributed that land, most recently in bits of ex-
colonial Africa. When property meant stocks and shares
and the ownership of enterprises, some governments
went out of their way to encourage more of their citizens
to take up the shareholding habit. Alternatively, some
governments sought to persuade them that nationaliza-
tion was one way to give all citizens a stake in the property of the nation.

Now that intelligence has replaced land as the
source of wealth, we have to take seriously that opening
sentence of *A Nation at Risk*, the 1983 report on American
education: "All, regardless of race or class or economic
status, are entitled to a fair chance and to the tools for developing their individual powers of mind and spirit to the

utmost." If we don't make this new property more widely available, if we don't invest in the intelligence of all our citizens, we shall have a divided society.

You can already see that divide deepening. Robert Reich has divided the modern American workforce into three categories. First, there are the routine operators, who are still needed to pack the airline meals, operate the tills, and put the data onto the discs. They make up perhaps one-quarter of the labor force, a proportion which is declining as their jobs get automated or are exported to lands with cheaper labor. Second, there are the personal service providers in restaurants, hospitals, and security firms, 30% and growing. Third, there are those people whom Reich calls the symbolic analysts, those who deal with numbers and ideas, problems, and words. They are the journalists, financial analysts, consultants, architects, lawyers, doctors, managers—those whose intelligence is their source of power and influence. They now make up perhaps 20% of all workers. Farmers, miners, and government employees make up the rest. It is the symbolic analysts, the knowledge workers, the professionals and the managers, who are the real beneficiaries of the information age because they own the new property.

Under present policies this "fortunate fifth" is getting richer almost by the minute, while the others get poorer. Reich calculates that in 1989 this top fifth had a higher after-tax income than the other four-fifths combined. In times gone by the rich had a vested interest in supporting the poor—in the final analysis the poor were both their customers and their neighbors—but the new rich sell their stuff to each other or to other firms, internationally. They do not venture downtown, use public transport, or send their children to the public schools. Why then, they say, should they pay more to support more of such things? They do not benefit themselves, even indirectly.

The conventional wisdom has been, both in the United States and Europe, that the private sector pays for the public sector. Help the private sector to get rich and the other sector will benefit. Selfishness makes sense. That was true when property was the old-fashioned sort—land, bricks, and machinery. Wealth did trickle down. More of that sort of property needed more people to work it. Intelligence as property changes that beneficial sequence. The causal chain is reversed; a rich private sector no longer results in a richer public sector, it's the other way around. Without investment in the public sector, in housing, in telecommunications and transport, and, most of all, in education, the number of symbolic analysts cannot increase significantly, the stock of useful intelligence will remain confined to one-fifth of the population. The other people will be progressively cut off from the world of property in the new sense, increasingly poor and effectively disenfranchised.

THE NATURE
OF INTELLIGENCE

If intelligence is the new basis of property and wealth, it is odd that we aren't always more eager to grab more of it. In Britain, nearly three out of ten youngsters leave full-time school as soon as they can, at 16, without any qualifications and often without an educational certificate in any subject. By contrast, in Germany, Japan, the Netherlands, France, and America, 90% stay in school or formal training until at least 18. In America, however, it may not do them all that much good. As the Education Committee of Congress discovered, fewer than 4 in 10 young adults can summarize in writing the main argument of a news column. Only 25 out of 100 young adults can use a bus schedule to work out how to get from here to there at a particular time. Only 10% can select the least costly product from a list of grocery items on the basis of unit-pricing information. Something isn't working as it should. Either the young are short-sighted and stupid or, just possibly, they are right—they don't feel that they are learning what they should while they are there, not in Britain or America, at any rate. It is not, they may instinctively feel, the right sort of intelligence in which to invest.

Consider, on the other hand, this question from an entrance paper to Tokyo University:

> Given a regular pyramid V with a square base, there is a ball with its centre on the bottom of the pyramid and tangent to all edges. If each length of the pyramid base is of length a, find the following quantities: (1) the height of V; (2) the volume of the portion common to the ball and pyramid.

How many of our students applying to study math at a university would be happy to tackle this problem on their way in? The snag is—this was not a question in the math entrance exam, it was in the paper for humanities students! The academic standards are high in Japan. Nonetheless, when these sophisticated learners start work, they have to start learning all over again. Japanese businesses see the universities as a recruiting ground, not an education. As they used to say of Oxford, it only needs to run a recruitment office and a placement office; what happens in between is irrelevant.

The Japanese themselves worry that their educational system is no longer preparing people adequately for a complex and shifting world. Other countries are also puzzled as to how best to deliver this new form of property. Intelligence may be the source of wealth, power, and freedom, but, inconveniently, real intelligence is not a substance, it cannot be pre-packaged, sorted, and delivered as if it were a consumer product. Some elements of it can, it is true; intelligence defined as information can be treated in just that way, it can be pre-packaged, disseminated, stored, and retrieved; it can be mass produced, made consumer-friendly, distributed in multimedia, and tested for reception. It is very tempting to think that when that form of intelligence has been dispersed, the job has been done. But to know all is not to be able to do all.

I have long admired Howard Gardner's concept of multiple intelligences, as described in his book *Frames of Mind.* He lists seven intelligences and describes how they can be measured. He arrived at his theory by watching brain-damaged patients. Some had a normal intelligence but could not remember their personal history, or recognize faces, even their own. Others could do everything except count. The important conclusion is that none of the intelligences is necessarily connected with any other. You can be as bright as a button in one and a dunce in another. You can shine in five or only in two. My own list has *nine* different forms of intelligence:

- Factual intelligence, the intelligence demonstrated by the human encyclopedia who wins the Mastermind competitions in Britain, who knows the answer to every question in Trivial Pursuit, and can give an impromptu lecture on the state of the Rumanian economy over dinner. We are envious but often bored.

- Analytical intelligence, the intelligence which thrives on intellectual problems, crosswords, and puzzles. People who score high on this intelligence delight in reducing complex data to more simple formulations. Strategic consultants, scientists, and academics are also strong in this type of intelligence. When this intelligence is combined with factual intelligence, examinations come easy. When we describe someone as an intellectual it is often this combination we have in mind.

- Linguistic intelligence, seen in the person who speaks seven languages and can pick up another within a month. I envy such people since I don't have this facility myself, but we have to remember that it is not necessarily connected with the first two intelligences.

- Spatial intelligence, the intelligence that sees patterns in things. Artists have it, as do mathematicians and systems designers. Entrepreneurs have it in dollops, but without necessarily having the other intelligences, which explains why many an entrepreneur would never go near a business school.

- Musical intelligence, the sort that gave Mozart his genius, but that also drives pop stars and their bands, many of whom would never have had a chance of going to college, because their scores on the first two intelligences would have been too low.

- Practical intelligence, the intelligence that allows young kids to take a motor bike apart and put it together again, although they might not be able to explain why in words. Many "intellectuals," intelligent in the first two senses of the word, are notoriously impractical and unworldly. "Am in Crewe," Chesterton cabled his wife. "Where should I be?"

- Physical intelligence, the intelligence, or talent, that we can see in sport stars, which enables some to hit balls much better than others, to ski better, dance better, and generally coordinate mind and muscle in ways that defeat me.

- Intuitive intelligence, the gift that some have of seeing things that others can't, even if they cannot explain why or wherefore. It is said that women have this intelligence to a greater degree than men, which may be why men often disparage it.

- Interpersonal intelligence, the wit and the ability to get things done with and through other people. Notoriously, this intelligence often does not go with analytical or information intelligence. "Too clever by half," the jibe aimed at the Conservative politician, Ian MacLeod, in years gone by, to explain why he would never be the great leader he could have been, applies to others as well. Without this form of intelligence, great minds can be wasted.

My list is based on observation. There may be more than nine types of intelligence. The important point is that intelligence has many faces, all of them useful, all of them potential property in this new world. We will not all be symbolic analysts in the future, but we will all have to create and manage our own work doughnuts. To do that we need to have a clear idea of our best intelligences, and have learned to make the most of them. It may be more an article of faith than a researchable fact, but we should make the starting assumption, in a just society, that *everyone* is intelligent in at least one of the nine ways. It should, then, be the first duty of any school to discover one's intelligence(s) and develop it (them). "Know Yourself," said Juvenal, were words given from the gods and inscribed on the ancient temple of Delphi. An impossible precept, grumbled Carlyle, it should be replaced by the more nearly possible, "know what you can work at."

THE THREE
C's

Discovering your intelligences is one thing, applying them is another. We need to be able to recognize and identify problems and opportunities. We need to be able to organize ourselves and other people to do something about them, and we need to be able to sit back and reflect on what has happened in order that we can do it all better the next time around. It is the cycle of discovery at work.

The skills involved are conceptualizing, coordinating, and consolidating—the three c's. They are the "verbs" of education as opposed to the "nouns," the "doing" words, not the facts. We don't learn to use these verbs by sitting in rows in a classroom, but by practice. Without them we may be a potential Nobel prize-winner or a star athlete but no one, least of all ourselves, will ever find out. These three c's should be the core of any educational doughnut. Unfortunately, they seldom are; instead they are regarded as add-ons, optional skills for what space is left in the doughnut. That is why Japanese businesses have to re-educate their clever new recruits as soon as they arrive. That is why some kids may be right to leave school early; they will learn the three c's more quickly on the streets.

I asked a professor of English at Cambridge University what they did there to educate his students for the demanding and prestigious jobs which most of this talented group would surely move on to in life. That, he said, was no business of his. "They come here to read English, and that is exactly what they do." Tony Benn once listed his education in *Who's Who* as taking place "in the intervals between terms at Westminster School and Oxford." He may have been right. The children of the symbolic analysts learn the three c's as they grow up, mentored and coached by their elders as effectively as the new recruits are in the Japanese firms. Their parentage thus accentuates their advantages.

A just, and sensible, society will do something about that accumulating difference between the children of the successful and the others. Since 80% of the young do not have symbolic analysts as parents, we have no choice but to use their early schooling as a substitute. That means intensive care and attention in the years from 4 to 10, when the c skills are beginning to be formed. At present, in Britain, there are 25 children to every teacher at this level, but only 10 students per teacher at the undergraduate level. We ought to reverse the ratios.

If they were properly educated at the start, students ought to be able to take responsibility for more of their own learning at the university level, something which they are unfairly expected to do at the primary stage. When it is argued that there is no evidence to show that class size at the primary level affects learning, I have to point out that what is being measured in that research is the retention of information or the acquisition of repetitive skills, the nouns. The verbs, as we know from trying to develop them in adult life in organizations, need mentoring, small-group experience, and real-life problem solving. You have to live them to learn them.

With ten small children to a teacher it is possible to approximate the kind of real-time, real-life learning that the children of the symbolic analysts pick up. With ten children it is possible to move between the classroom and life outside in a way that is not logistically possible with 25. It can be any ten children. There is a lot of piecemeal evidence to suggest that you do not have to be the child of a symbolic analyst to learn these things. Most people can do it if they start young enough.

In a famous program in America Jaime Escalante got low-income Hispanic students through the advanced placement examination in calculus, one of those conceptual subjects normally restricted to the so-called brightest in the class. If he could do that with one of the toughest of noun skills, there is no saying what he might have done with the verb skills. What small groups and close mentoring and learning from life can do, and which large classes can rarely do, is to give a child self-confidence.

PORTFOLIOS
AT SCHOOL

We could go further. Instead of requiring students to reach certain standards before they receive their certificate, we could require *the school* to ensure that the student has reached those standards before they let them go. School should be a place for compiling a portfolio of competences. Those competences need not, and should not, be age linked, with levels or tests or examinations to be passed at particular ages, because people learn these verb skills at very different paces. Like music tests or driving tests they should be taken when one is ready for them and likely to pass. If every 16-year-old takes the same examination at the same time, and if that examination is graded, half of the population will, inevitably and logically, do better than the other half. The net effect is to persuade half of the population that they are failures, however often you tell them that they have passed.

Wherever we need tests we must make a distinction

between age and competence, and allow retakes of everything. Ultimately, almost everyone everywhere passes their driving test. My daughter passed hers at 18, my son at 24, because he was not in a hurry to learn to drive. Neither of them, now, a year later, thinks that they are a better or worse driver than the other. If everyone took the same driving test at 18, and only the top half were considered competent to drive, we should have fewer, better drivers and safer roads. We should also have a lot of very deprived and discontented people, including many who might well have developed into very competent drivers a few years later.

If the age bonding of our schools went on throughout life, we should be very resentful. If only 25-year-olds could take the accounting examinations or only 39-year-olds apply for full professorships, there would be an outcry. It can only be for reasons of administrative convenience that schools remain the most agist of all our institutions.

Students should each be required to compile a bulging portfolio of certificates of competence or achievement. Apart from certificates of competence in the traditional subjects, I see no reason why driving, swimming, first aid, word processing, cooking, tax law, telephone and presentation skills, and any other practical life skills should not be certificated and collected during this period of life. These are certificates of competence. They can be formally tested, as with music or driving, or they can be examined on the evidence of their work, as with artists' portfolios.

This form of portfolio collection should and does go on throughout life, but the habit needs to be acquired when young. It will be an essential part of the portfolio life we are all going to experience at one stage or another. Even inside the organization, as I have argued, portfolios will be the way people develop their careers, with the organization encouraging them to add to their credentials at every level, sometimes by new accredited experience, sometimes by certificated tests or courses. The Records of Achievement which are becoming increasingly common in British schools are a step in the direction of portfolio collections. To be effective they need to become part of a nationally accepted scheme of educational portfolios, not the icing on the cake that they are today, a sop for those who cannot excel at the traditional examinations. When we make all examinations age-independent and when we happily include certificates relating to all the intelligences, we shall begin to see a proper balance in our education system.

There is, however, no need for all this portfolio collection to take place *in* school although it should happen while *at* school. The school can and should be the organizing hub for all the extra-curricular activity. There is no reason why subjects like languages, computer skills, or domestic science should not be taught by specialist agencies, under the general supervision of the school.

If the education service is unwilling to see its role so enlarged, we should develop a separate youth service which takes over where the formal schooling leaves off, handling all the sports, work experience, and community activities as well as the more practical aspects of the portfolio. School proper might end, as on the Continent, at 2 p.m. when the youth service would take over, staffed by some full-time professionals but with the help of many part-timers, voluntary workers or parents, portfolio people themselves.

It could go even further. Technology, and the possibilities of multimedia, will make independent learners of us all. There is no reason why some may not choose to learn for themselves, by themselves, in some topics, presenting themselves for examination when they are ready, rather as one already does for a driving test. The function of the school, or the youth service, would be to act as a tracking station to make sure that no one was falling through the net, or losing the benefits and lessons of the three c's. The school would then be the core of an educational doughnut organization. Some teachers would be core staff, well paid for long hours and flexibility. Others would be specialists, working outside the core and selling their expertise to a range of schools or institutions. Some would move between the two roles during their career.

THE DOUBLE BOND

Portfolios and the doughnut school may not be enough. We learn about life from life and we learn about work through working, mixed with a judicious amount of coaching, teaching, and reflection. The German model of a blend of workplace experience and formal instruction for all but the most academic at age 16 has been widely admired and is beginning to be imitated in many countries with subtle national variations. There is always a danger that this is a recipe, in a changing world, for training people in jobs and skills that will soon be obsolete. Unfortunately, if you go along with curvilinear logic, all is ultimately obsolete.

This kind of learning must, therefore, be complemented by some of that verb learning, which might, in a sensible world, have been learned earlier but probably won't have been. We should, therefore, present every young person on adulthood, at age 18, with a double bond. One part of that bond would guarantee to pay the fees, up to a defined level, with basic maintenance, for two years or the equivalent of full-time study at any recognized learning institution. This part of the bond could be used at any stage of one's life. There would be no age barrier. It would be up to the individual to apply and up to the institution to accept or reject them. The state would guarantee payment but not admission. The assumption would be that sufficient institutions would create themselves to meet this demand once it was seen to be underwritten to this extent.

This part of the double bond would automatically be taken up by those who go on to the university. They would, therefore, get the first two years of their higher education free. If the course lasted longer than two years, they would have to pay for the extra time. At present, first-degree courses in Britain are three or four years' long. If the proposal of a double bond were introduced there, we might expect to see the first degree compressed into two fuller years, to be followed by an optional two years of graduate study. These graduate years could be paid for by a graduate tax on future earnings. Those who earn less would then, automatically, have more years in which to pay it off. It is fair.

The other part of the double bond would be a guarantee to find a full-time job for any citizen who wanted one, for two years locally, either in a voluntary organization or in a government agency, at a level equivalent to the minimum wage, where one exists. It would be a recognition that there are many things about life and work that you can only learn by working and living—the verb skills in particular. The government would run what would, in effect, be an employment agency in each region. Since this would be labor in excess of the requirements of the labor market, the jobs would have to be located in the voluntary sector or in nonstatutory government work where they did not substitute for longer-term jobs and workers. The two bonds could be used in conjunction, if the individual so wished and could so arrange.

This double bond would be a manifestation of society's continued investment in every citizen when they reach adulthood, not just in those who see themselves on the academic track. In return, society would be entitled to refuse to support anyone until the two bonds had been used, realizing, however, that there would be exceptional circumstances in some individual cases. The double bond would be one way of providing the essential extra investment necessary to launch the individual into the intelligence society with the skills, both intellectual and practical, which he or she will need to survive.

Although only a minority of people would cash in their bonds, although the bonds would effectively replace many welfare payments, and although work would be done in the community that might not otherwise be affordable, the scheme would, potentially, cost a lot of money. It would have to be seen as an investment in the long-term future. Its payoff would come in the reduced need to provide for these people in later life, if they were better able to look after themselves. It would come, indirectly, in the lower costs of policing and repairing a more contented and just society. If Singapore thinks it right to invest 25% of her GDP in education, training, and development, the rest of us should be able to do at least as well. It is naive to think that learning for life can finish at 16 or even 18, yet that is the implicit message which we are giving today to many of our young.

Learning, like life, goes on forever. It would be reasonable to expect that the workplace would see the good sense of investing in intelligence, at least for its core workforce. We would be often disappointed. Too many organizations do not think far enough ahead to wait for the payoff from the investment. Others hope to cash in on other people's investment and entice their educated and trained staff to join them. Some rely on the individuals to invest in themselves. Some compromise is needed if learning is to become the fashion throughout life.

One way to encourage the fashion would be to set a legal benchmark for organizations, requiring them to spend a set percentage of their payroll on education and training, a figure to be reported in their audited accounts. Any organization falling below the standard would forfeit the difference to a central training fund. The French require 1.2% of the payroll to be spent in this way. Most firms exceed it. With the minimum of bureaucracy a minimum level is thus established, but to set the level at 0.5%, as the British Labour Party recently proposed, is to underestimate the investment required in the age of intelligence. My university requires that an average of one day a week be spent on research, keeping ahead of my subject. That is 20% of my time. One half of that—10%—might be a minimum standard for anyone in the years ahead. Five days a year, the norm for good employers, leaves a large gap to be filled.

Some of this money and time could be seen as the entitlement of the individuals, to invest in their own development as they thought fit. The organization does not necessarily or always know what is best for one. If an individual is entitled to annual holidays, sick leave, and maternity leave, it seems only sensible to extend the entitlement to intelligence. The slogan of some American corporations, "individual initiative and corporate support," has the right ring to it, but is usually interpreted only to mean attendance at some selected courses. It needs wider application, a guaranteed sum of money per annum, accumulated for up to seven years if need be.

It is, however, the outsiders who are most likely to miss out on continuous investment in developing their intelligence. Most organizations will leave it up to the individual, and most of those will be too poor, too busy, or too short-sighted to do it for themselves. Here lies the biggest danger of the intelligence age, a diminishing competence at the bottom end of the labor market. Outsiders need help.

THE NEW AGENTS

All independents need an agent. A good half of us will be independents at any one time in the future, and all of us will be independent at one stage or another. Independents are never unemployed, officially—they just have no work. Resting, they call it in the theatrical world. If the unemployment figures eventually decline in Europe, it will, in part, be because many people will perforce have gone independent. To make their portfolios bigger and better they will need an agent. While some independents will have bulging portfolios and full diaries, many will be among the most vulnerable of our societies' unprotected, unwanted, deteriorating assets. That will further no one's interest.

Actors and models have agents, writers have agents as do golfers, tennis players, and boxers. It is hard enough to market and price yourself when you are a star; it is impossible when no one knows you and when you are unsure of what you can offer. A good agent will not only find buyers for your talents and negotiate the deal, he or she will be a coach or mentor, helping you review your experience and guiding you to appropriate educational opportunities. Good agents will prod your creativity by floating ideas in front of you: "Have you ever considered . . . ?" or "Would this sort of thing interest you . . . ?" They will suggest what you need to do or where you need to go to improve your skills or to enlarge your experience.

They will also, if they are any good, help organize your schedule. This is not altruism. It is in their interest to increase the value of the asset they are managing. It is, for the independent, a great comfort to know that there is someone whose interests entirely coincide with theirs, because it can be a lonely world outside the organization. There is a growing market for agents of portfolio workers. The executive leasing agencies have been quick to move in to the upper end of that market. They provide executives or project managers to organizations to cover short-term skill gaps. They are, in effect, agents for portfolio executives.

The need is critical for those lower down the skill range. This would have been a natural opportunity for the old trade unions, whose membership and influence has inevitably waned as the minimalist organization has waxed. The unions have been noticeably reluctant to recognize this new market. Therefore we must look to new intermediaries. It would be nice if the employment agencies were more than brokers, and lived up to their name and act as agents, not of employers, but of the individual. If they were far-sighted enough, it would pay them to spend money upgrading the skills and the knowledge of those on their books in order to increase the rates they could then demand from the hiring organization. Some already offer training opportunities, more must follow suit.

Portfolio workers need more than agents, they need somewhere where they belong. Learning is alienating if you do it all by yourself. Teleworking is fine in theory but lonely in reality. That asset which is yourself can atrophy in isolation. We independents need somewhere other than the home, a place where there are colleagues, not clients, where we can find the companionship and gossip of the old office or factory but without the boss. Somewhere where we can exchange experience and contacts. We need a club. I have argued, earlier, that the hub of the minimalist organization will be a clubhouse for the members of the dispersed core. It should also be available to key portfolio workers to use when they need it. One piece of everyone's portfolio should, if possible, include the use of a club facility as part of the fee. For the many who cannot negotiate that privilege, I would like to see employment agencies offer a similar facility in exchange for an exclusive right to sell your skills.

As the portfolio market becomes more competitive, we may see these new intermediaries actually employing a reserve labor force which they sell on, keeping the risks and rewards for themselves. The portfolio worker would have to trade some freedom for more security, a guarantee of training and traditional employee benefits such as holiday pay and sick leave. Some organizations, Hewlett-Packard in France for one, IBM in London for another, do something of the sort for their newly redundant or retired workers, putting them on retainer or a guaranteed-fee basis for a certain proportion of their time. They have created clubs that pay you to belong, but to keep your membership you have to keep your skills up to date, you have to continue growing your asset.

Some portfolio workers form their own clubs or networks. Networks are useful, but if they reside mainly in your address files, they lack the spontaneity of a club. It is not quite the same as a bar and a reading room. Every network needs a club at its hub to add the human face to the electronic impulse. Clubs for the unemployed offer the right facilities but can, too often, be places of shared misery rather than shared learning. Only if their members start to think portfolio does the club take on a new life, looking not for jobs but for customers.

The independent workers of our societies are among the most vulnerable and the least protected. Europe's Social Charter is an attempt to remedy that, but will probably be more often honored in the breach than in the observance. Britain's refusal to sign it may only be the more honorable face of noncompliance. In a competitive world, with a surplus of labor sloshing around, independents will need all the help they can get. It is in all our interests to give it to them.

11 *The New Scorecard*

McNamara was, unfortunately, right. He said, in what has come to be known as the McNamara Fallacy:

> The first step is to measure whatever can be easily measured. This is OK as far as it goes. The second step is to disregard that which can't be easily measured or to give it an arbitrary quantitative value. This is artificial and misleading. The third step is to presume that what can't be measured easily really isn't important. This is blindness. The fourth step is to say that what can't be easily measured really doesn't exist. This is suicide.

What does not get counted does not count. Money is easily counted. Therefore, all too soon, money becomes the measure of all things. A just society needs a new scorecard.

THE DISTORTIONS
OF MONEY

The idea of national income accounting, on a regular standardized basis, the GDP and the GNP numbers which we all now assume is what we mean by "national income," is really quite a new idea. In Britain it started in 1940 when the government, helped and advised by Keynes, needed to work out how much money it could raise in order to fight the war. Before then there had only been occasional and nonstandardized estimates. My first job with my oil company was in Singapore, where, by default, I, trained in classical history and philosophy, was appointed their first "regional economist." I was asked to prepare a series of forecasts relating oil consumption to national income, drawing on ratios established elsewhere in the world. Unfortunately there were no national income statistics for Singapore. This was in 1956, when it was still a British colony. I may have been the first to make a very rough and inadequate estimate of Singapore's GDP, an estimate which, I recall, involved guessing at the earnings of Singapore's prostitutes.

Things are different now. Singapore is proud to boast of her per capita income. League tables of national income proliferate. It is assumed that these equate with standards of living, but the statistics measure only the visible transfers of money. So, for instance, and most notoriously, they don't measure the unpaid work in the home. If, however, the wife dies and her husband hires someone to do the work which she did for nothing, the apparent prosperity of the country would rise by the £18,000 which the Legal and General Insurance Company say it will cost in the 1990s. Voluntary and charitable work, gift work, is not included because no money changes hands, nor is the caring for the elderly if it is done for love or compassion in one's own home. Put your parents in a home for the elderly, however, and society is immediately the richer, statistically.

More insidiously, if the cars and the highways are so bad that accidents proliferate, then hospital, car repair, and insurance bills increase, and so does the supposed wealth of the country as these transactions find their way into the national accounts. You can spend money polluting the clean air of the countryside with a factory, muck up its rivers, and destroy the peace and the stillness of the place, and it will all be counted as an increase in wealth because nothing is deducted for the damage. If the firm were fined, or charged, for what they had done it would make us even richer. We are encouraged to be a disposable society by the way we count. The more you throw things away and buy new things instead of having them repaired, the richer the society appears.

The distortions go on. Leisure, that precious commodity, only gets counted if you spend money on it. I have sometimes, half jokingly, suggested that the reason that the Germans are richer than the British is because the Germans tend to live in apartments while the British like their homes to have gardens. If you live in an apartment, every time you go out you will, normally, either spend money or make money. Meanwhile the Britisher goes into the garden and watches the cucumber growing, or weeds the flower bed. No money, so no wealth. Love is for free, so buy diamonds instead—it will make the country richer. Don't cook her a meal, take her to a restaurant instead. Don't make music, buy music. Riding the bullet train from Tokyo to Osaka through hundreds of miles of desolate industrial landscape, I have to remind myself that the people who live there are richer than most Europeans. They don't always think so. In one survey the Japanese who were questioned reckoned that they had, in reality, a lower quality of life than every European country except for Portugal.

Adding up all the financial transactions by all the companies and institutions in a country, converting it to dollars and dividing it by the number of people in a society does not tell you how comfortable they are. Cold climates have to spend more money than warm ones. In Britain, if you want hot sun or cold snow, it gets expensive. In Italy they have these things for nothing. Poor Italians! Income is not equally distributed between people or between organizations and people; Japan keeps more of its money inside its organizations than Britain does; aging societies spend more than young societies and have fewer people. They look richer, but can feel poorer.

When the IMF used purchasing power parities (PPPs) instead of the normal market exchange rates, to compare the output of countries, it found that China, for instance, went from $370 per head to $2,460, and India from $275 to $1,255. A little money goes a long way in China and India. PPPs reflect that fact. The $370 was clearly unreal when 70% of Chinese urban households have color television and 80% have washing machines. When the IMF added up the output of all the countries of the developing world on this new basis, it discovered that the developing world's share of the world's output had jumped from 18% to 34%, and that of the industrial world had fallen from 73% to 54%. China, in fact, because of its population, is, on a PPP basis, the second richest country in the world, after the United States and above Japan. The way you see things depends on the way you count them.

There have also been attempts to add some of the invisibles to the visible. The World Economic Forum in Switzerland produces an annual league table which assesses a wide range of factors such as Infrastructure, Science and Technology, and People as well as Domestic Economic Strength to rank the 22 OECD countries and 15 newly industrialized nations on economic competitiveness. In 1992, Japan came out on top by a wide margin, followed by the United States. Britain lagged behind at sixteenth place. Most countries estimate their informal, "black," economies; one or two add this estimate into their national income. In one year, 1987, Italy surpassed Britain in the international league table when she did this, adding 18% to her GNP in one key stroke of a statistician's computer. No one has yet added home work or gift work to the numbers but that time might not be far off. It would be a painless way to get rich quicker and would benefit Britain with her long tradition of voluntary work. Therefore, we should remember the principle that no one set of numbers can ever serve all purposes. What we need are two sets of national accounts, one recording the money transactions and one listing all the other indicators of life.

COUNTING
INVISIBLES

This second list would include health and death statistics, infant mortality, age of death, cause of death. It would include education numbers, employment numbers, and statistics on other forms of work; there would be details of housing, of environmental indicators such as carbon dioxide emissions, deforestation, and energy use, and of more subjective indicators such as people's feelings about their quality of life. All these numbers currently exist in most countries. In Britain, many of them are published annually in documents such as *Social Trends*, which has its equivalent elsewhere. What we need is not a new system of national accounts as much as a companion set of national statistics which can be compared year by year and country by country. The UN's International Comparison Program, which attempts to do some of this, may yet turn out to be one of the more important of its initiatives.

The statistics collected, we need to give the numbers on the second list the same sort of public prominence we give to the money figures. They should, for instance, be presented as an annual review to every Parliament or Congress, be debated and discussed in the media, and contrasted, for celebration or lament, with the statistics of other countries. Over time they would provide benchmarks for a civilized society, to run alongside the national income figures. Both sets of figures are necessary if what we count affects the way we behave, and if we want a more balanced and just society.

We could start the reforms by making the national income accounts a little more honest. Governments run the country on a cash-flow basis, "money in" versus "money out" each year. The difference is the deficit, or what the British quaintly call the Public Sector Borrowing Requirement. This allows them to take no account of the difference between an investment and an expenditure—they are both outgoing, even though the investment may save money in the future whereas the expenditure is gone for good. Education, therefore, is always a cost and never an investment. The cash-flow convention allows them to sell assets and call it revenue, even though it will never be repeated. The same convention allows them to treat bonanzas, such as Britain's North Sea oil production in the 1980s, which was never going to last very long, as an addition to revenue rather than the equivalent of Aunt Agatha's legacy, a one-time bounty, something to be invested in one's future.

The result is distorted priorities. There is no incentive to think long term. There is no way to trade an expenditure today against savings or benefits in the future. There is no need to take account of future liabilities; the costs of not maintaining roads and railways, or unfunded state pension schemes. If we behaved that way in our own lives, we would never buy a house, we would run our cars until they fell apart, and we would spend the minimum on our children's education because the long-term future would always come second to paying the bills. In our private lives we get around that problem by turning large lumps of investment, such as a house, into smaller streams of expenditure, by means of a loan or a mortgage. If we are wise, we borrow only to finance future investment, not to cover the monthly bills. Government muddles them up. No business wants to behave like that, nor would it be allowed to. Politicians have always and consistently resisted the pressure to do their accounts in a proper business-like way, arguing that it would tie their hands unnecessarily and that, one way or another, they have to finance both the running deficit and the capital expenditure by borrowing, so why separate them out artificially?

One country, however, has made an attempt to be business-like and to present a proper balance. New Zealand produced a national balance sheet for the first time in 1991. It revealed that its assets—state companies, roads, lands and buildings, financial reserves, and investments—totalled NZ$14.4 billion less than its liabilities, by which it meant its borrowings at home and abroad and its pension liabilities. Technically, the country was bankrupt. Realistically, it means that future taxpayers will have to pay for the relative profligacy of their predecessors. New Zealand will continue to publish its old cash-flow accounts but the new "business" accounts will help show how well the present and the future are balanced. *The Economist* calculated that, using these sorts of figures, the net worth of New Zealand Inc. had deteriorated by $12 billion dollars over the past 20 years. By not counting, you could say, the New Zealanders had mortgaged their future. The present system of government accounting in other countries allows expediency to flourish because no one knows the true costs. Better counting would allow a more informed debate about the longer-term balance of priorities and would bring the issue of national purpose and direction to the surface.

A SCORECARD
FOR BUSINESS

Companies may have better balance sheets than governments but they, too, have a long way to go. They do not normally count or communicate:

- The intellectual assets of the company (including brands, patents, skill base)
- Expenditures on the enhancement of these assets, including

    R&D training and development
    The introduction of new products or services
    Employee morale and productivity

- The customer

    Quality of goods and service
    Customer satisfaction

- The environment

    Investment and expenditure on environmental control and improvement

Expenditure on community work
Investment in the community

These things are difficult to count and in themselves mean nothing. It is only when you start to compare last year with this year, or your company with your competitors, that the numbers get interesting. Comparison provides the benchmarks. Without any sort of numbers, however, the cash-flow numbers are the ones that count. It is hard to know whether the business is in proper balance, whether the future is receiving the right resources, and whether the stakeholders' requirements are in balance. If, as an investor or a customer, you are betting on the intellectual property of the concern, you will need more than historical money numbers.

William Reilly, when administrator of America's Environmental Protection Agency, was asked what the Eastern Europeans should do first in the long haul to clean up the massive pollution in their countries. He replied:

> My answer is to begin with the disclosure of emissions. Require that the data be published in the local newspapers. Then support a healthy nongovernmental, environmental movement. At that point a fascinating dynamic will begin to occur: the community will interact with plant managers, workers and government to reduce pollution levels. Such is the power of information.

Counting it makes it visible, and counting makes it count.

IBM now measures each of its "Baby Blues" on seven parameters: four financial numbers (revenue growth, profit, return on assets, and cash flow) and three new measures (customer satisfaction, quality, and employee morale). In Britain, Dr. David Budworth is exploring the concept of an "innovation ratio," relating the amount spent on innovation (research and development, training, and the development of brands) to the value-added by the company. Others are looking for ways to measure a company's "knowledge bank." Some already do it in their published accounts under the heading of "intangible assets." The trouble is that you have to read the very small print in the notes to the accounts to find out what this means. Because they are measured in different ways they will mean different things to different firms. To a publisher it means the publishing rights it holds. To WPP, the communications firm, it meant the brands of their two big advertising agencies, J. Walter Thompson and Ogilvie Benson Mather. It did not say how it had valued them, but it was, at least, a recognition that intellectual capital had a value.

Putting estimates of intellectual assets on the balance sheet may, however, only confuse matters. If we give them money numbers, we shall be trying, once again, to use one set of numbers to count different sorts of things. Just as we use different measures for liquids and solids, so we should happily use different measures for each stakeholder. For the environment, for instance, the United Nations initiative suggests that each organization should include in its annual report:

- the organization's environmental policy

- the capitalization of environmental expenditures

- any environmental liabilities such as bringing the organization into line with new regulations

- disclosure of other anticipated environmental expenditure

The Pearce Report for the British government would, if it were ever acted upon, require organizations to disclose their man-made, natural, and critical capital assets and the costs of maintaining them. Other possibilities are a mandatory environmental audit to monitor observance with environmental standards or a full energy-accounting system.

These are just a sample of the numbers being looked at. As a result of these new numbers, the environmental movement is in danger of consuming more forests through measuring the forests it is saving. The environmental cleaning business is now thought to be worth over $60 billion in the United States alone, and growing. The bigger the problem, the bigger the business. Germany is estimated to have nearly 40% of the Eastern European environmental market. If you turn the problem into a business the numbers will appear.

Consumer needs are another growing business. Sensible businesses recognize that contented customers are faithful customers and will run surveys, collect data, and analyze repeat buys. As more organizations realize that they are businesses even if they don't have shareholders, the practice is spreading. Britain's hospitals have started a customer response record, to keep track of how satisfied their patients feel with their treatment. So are prisons. Neither hospitals nor prisons want their customers to come back so they have to turn the repeat business statistics upside down. Big numbers are bad. Comparing their nonrepeat business with their peer institutions across the country is a valuable benchmark. They have, at the very least, to explain why they are different. Different numbers set different agendas.

For a proper balance organizations need to audit their relationships with all their stakeholders, even if some of the details should remain confidential. There would be no damage in publishing details of a firm's involvement with the community, or its investment in its people. One sign of the changing priorities of the times is the number of firms that see some competitive advantage in advertising their activities in this field instead of merely reporting them. "Join us," advertized one accounting firm, "and we will invest at least ten percent of your salary in your development each year." "We promise every employee the chance to work one day a month in the community at our cost," declared another. If it is seen as a business opportunity, the numbers emerge. Details of intellectual property or supplier relationships may be more private, although audited general ratios, such as an innovation ratio, would give nothing away to competitors but would be an indication of the level of investment in the long-term capacity of the organization. These could and should be public.

Many boards of large companies have separate audit committees for social policy, for ethics, for remuneration, and for the environment. Some, such as ICI in Britain, publish a separate environmental report with their annual report. It is another recognition of the hexagon, of the variety of interest groups and of the multiple contradictions involved in charting the path of a business. It will be better still when we can make the data public, on a standard basis. In France a social audit is required as part of the annual report. My guess is that something similar will soon be required of all European companies. They will resent the bureaucracy and the costs involved, they will chafe at the restrictions on their freedom of action, but by counting the invisibles they will better balance the present against the future and the interest groups against one another. Sometimes, it seems, we have to be forced to be sensible. Once the playing field is level and the rules are known the game can start.

A PERSONAL SCORECARD

"How much money do you earn?" I used to ask my friends in my competitive days. It seemed the best way of comparing progress in life, after aiming off for the fact that I was then an oil executive while some of them were bustling bankers and others exhausted young doctors. I was brought up short by one who replied, "Enough." "What do you mean—enough?" I asked. "What I say—enough. I work out what I need and that's what I make sure I earn. Why bother to make more? How much sugar do you buy in a year?" he turned and asked me. "I have no idea," I said. "But I bet there's always sugar in your house when you need it. Money is like sugar, no point in hoarding it, it usually goes bad, or you have to make quite unnecessary cakes to use it up."

Crazy man, I thought; but as I grew older I realized the sense in what he had said. He was never rich but, as he said, "there was always sugar in the house" and he seemed much less harassed than the rest of us. But then he knew what he wanted out of life. He wasn't using money as a substitute for uncertainty. In a time of materialism most of the numbers are financial ones. The higher we score the more we earn, apparently, but like the sugar we then have to go out and spend the money we made, often on the equivalent of cakes which we don't really need. In the recession, many couples found that they were unable to trade up in the housing market as their families grew along with their income because they could find no buyer for their current home. "I was frustrated at first," one of them told me, "but then we said we've been very happy in this place; maybe it's a bit small and a bit un-smart, but that doesn't really matter. Let's go on enjoying what we've got and take the hassle out of life. We've got enough."

Money is seldom the measure of much, once you have enough. It is only the core of our personal doughnuts. I cannot be the only person to wonder what those people who are paid 1 million pounds or dollars in a year do with it all. Money isn't even necessarily the sign of success. In Britain the quickest way to get rich is to fail at the top. Sign a three-year contract and then fail in the first six months, walk away with a million pounds for six months' work. As I grew older I realized that my friends were not that impressed by those who had riches, as long as "there was sugar in the house."

SOME HINTS
OF CHANGE

If money is not the measure of all things, how do we put numbers on the other things—a walk in beautiful countryside, artistic expression, the love of a family, the joy of teaching, watching someone get well, the thrill of discovery, the satisfaction of a job well done, the delight of friends. We all know the taste of such things but find it hard to call them success. We need to find a way to list them even if we can't count them. We can learn a lot from our children, particularly when they grow into adults. I once asked my 24-year-old daughter what she thought she was doing with her life, dabbling in this and that, traveling, adventuring, socializing. "When," I said crossly, "are you going to find a proper career, make a serious contribution to this world?" She looked at me, a little pityingly, I thought. "There are many people," she said, "who rely on me for comfort and for help, who use me as their home. I learn something new each day, I laugh with someone every day, and I cook for someone almost every night. Oh, and I do no one any harm. I don't think that's bad for 24." I wondered how long it would be before I could say the same.

Laurence Shames, in his book *The Hunger for More: Searching for Values in an Age of Greed,* puts the dilemma this way:

> The frontier . . . is what has shaped the American way
> of doing things and the American sense of what's
> worth doing. . . . More money, more tokens of suc-
> cess—there will always be people for whom these are

adequate goals, but those people are no longer setting the tone for all of us. There is a sort of *more* at hand: more appreciation of good things beyond the marketplace, more insistence on fairness, more attention to purpose, more determination truly to choose a life, and not a lifestyle, for oneself. Dare we suggest that these new forms of *more* comprise a species of frontier?

Measuring more, he goes on to say, is easy, measuring better is hard.

Mickey Kraus, in America, shares my worries of a society increasingly divided because money is the measure of so much. He would like to take more things out of the market so that it did not matter whether you were rich or poor. The National Health Service in Britain does not differentiate between rich and poor. I am always relieved to land at Heathrow Airport after a trip abroad because I know that I can now afford to be seriously ill. Kraus would add the draft, or National Service, all schools and colleges, parks, and class-integrated housing. I would add public transport. His dream of a society that regarded a janitor as being "just as good as a banker because he works as hard" must be unrealistic, but the notion of taking as many things out of the money economy has much to commend it, expensive though it would be in taxes.

My own hope lies more in the denizens of the middle age of life, the increasingly long period beyond the job and before senility. Most of them will not have much chance to add more sugar to their store. Enough of that will have to be enough for them. They will begin to find that there are satisfactions and achievements which cannot be measured by money, that gift work and study work and home work can be richly rewarding. Because there are going to be a lot of such people they will be noticed. They will not be old, as we used to think of old, they will not be retired in the way their parents were retired, and most of them will not be poor. They will establish new case law, some new models for success, some new numbers. How many young people have you coached this year, they may inquire, how many paintings did you finish, how many gardens did you plant, how many books did you read or write? How many school trips did you organize, how many patients did you drive to the hospital, what moments of quiet beauty did you catch, which fireside chats have you treasured, what special meals did you prepare, how many friends did you advise, how many feuds did you settle?

Imagine one of those lambent June evenings in England, when the sun doesn't set until after nine, and the air is still and scented. I was walking along the riverbank in Cambridge, with immaculate lawns and the hauntingly beautiful chapel of King's College in front of me, when a snatch of treble voices in a choir floated over the trees and a young American couple stopped, entranced. "Remember this, honey," she said, "remember it always, this is quality time." If we are going to find a better balance in our lives and better justice in our societies, we need to find more examples of quality time, make them more accessible to more people, and make them count. We can do that by celebrating them more, for fashion is a powerful agent of change.

The Search for Meaning

Making Sense of Paradox

THE THREE SENSES

The Three Senses

"What is the point of it all?" a friend asked. "Why should we struggle with these second curves, doughnuts, and compromises? In the end, isn't life just a sick joke?" I knew how she felt. I had recently watched my wife's mother dying. One month she was the twinkly, irascible old lady at the heart of the family; the next she was a gray emasculated shape in a hospital bed, hardly able to smile, let alone talk. After that, nothing—a small pile of ashes in an urn. Could this be all there was to it?

For some there is no point. Chekhov said, "You ask me what life is? It is like asking what a carrot is. A carrot is a carrot." Maybe, as Gertrude Stein once said of Oakland, California, "There is no there there." We are all accidents in the evolutionary chain. We can lie back and enjoy it, or we can occupy ourselves, as scientists do, in trying to understand more about what is going on. There is nothing we can do to alter it, even when we understand it. We can only play with it. Man is as the smallest piece of dust in the universe. Descartes thought that animals were machines. Some biologists see no reason to think that humans are any different from animals.

This "myth of science" so frightened Allan Bloom when he saw the effect it was having on modern American youth that he wrote a best-selling book, *The Closing of the American Mind*. American college students, he observed, were not only lifeless and ignorant, they were reluctant to offer or to hold any opinions at all. People who thought that they were right in the past did terrible things as a result, therefore it is best to have no opinions at all. The only true knowledge is science. Everything else is wishful thinking. From that it follows that it is wrong to take a position on anything, worse still to try to impose your wishes on your bit of the world. A passive voyeurism will have to suffice, preferably uncritical and politically correct because it is wrong to suggest that any one way of life is superior to another.

That way lies a moral vacuum, where nothing is right and nothing really wrong. That way also lies inertia, no second curve, with compromises made for the wrong reasons. Immanuel Kant, then only a lecturer in philosophy in an obscure Prussian town in the eighteenth century, disagreed with Descartes. He sat down and wrote *Critique of Pure Reason* and made the world stop and think because in it he offered an alternative to the scientific arrogance which then, perhaps as now, held sway. Man, he maintained, was not a means to an end, he was himself the end. Man's life was driven and shaped by a moral pressure that came from within. There is something about the human condition that implies something religious, however we want to describe it. It is God in the human soul, Kant said, not God the architect of the scientific universe, who makes sense of who we are. "How do you know this?" he was asked. "Because of the moral force within me," he replied.

It is as good an answer as I know. Faith has no reasons. If there were reasons, or logic, there would be no need of faith. I cannot prove that there is a point to our existence. I agree with the philosopher Ludwig Wittgenstein who said, "Even when all the possible scientific questions have been answered, the problems of life remain completely untouched"; and with John Updike who said that existence felt like ecstasy, even if we were not able to describe it or define it. Even if it is a conceit, we feel that we know that we have something like a soul, that we matter, and that we are in some small way unique. There is a haunting passage in the Book of Revelation: "To anyone who prevails, the Spirit says, I will give a white stone, on which is written a new name which no one knows except he who receives it." I keep a white stone on my desk as a reminder of my uniqueness. Even if there is no point, even if it is all a game of science, we must still believe that there is a point. If we don't believe that, there is no reason to do anything, believe anything, change anything. The world would be at the mercy of those who did believe that they could change things. It is a risk we cannot take.

To find that reason for our doing and our being, it helps to build on three senses—*a sense of continuity, a sense of connection, and a sense of direction*. Without them we may feel disoriented and rudderless. The world is going to be a confusing place for the next few decades. We shall need all the help that we can get to recognize our place and role in it. These senses are the best antidote I know to the feelings of impotence which rapid change induces in us all.

12 *A Sense of Continuity*

A few years before he died, my father gave me a dirty brown envelope. "I'm never going to get round to this now," he said, "so you had better have it." It was a collection of old family papers, including a family tree going back two or three hundred years. I looked at it and noticed that there was a namesake of mine a few generations back, one Charles Handy, who was born in 1765 and died in 1836. He married and had four children, of whom two died early. One of the other two was my great-great-grandfather. That was all I knew. The paper told me nothing about where that first Charles Handy lived, what he did, how he looked, how rich he was, or whether he was a nice sort of chap—nothing. "Is that what will become of me?" I wondered, a name on a family tree to be looked at one hundred years hence by someone I know not of. Is that what it's all about? Why, then, I might as well make merry and die.

It was then that I, by chance, came across the last

few verses of the Book of Ruth. These are hardly famous verses; they consist entirely of a list of names: "Pharoz begat Hezron," it goes, "and Hezron begat Ram, and Ram begat Amminadab . . ." and so on for another six names, and then, conclusively, "and Jesse begat David." But that was the point; David was the point. He was the great king of the Jews, and the link, ultimately, with Jesus. Without those other people, there would have been no David; they were the essential links in the chain. Without that eighteenth century Charles Handy, I would not be today.

I realized, then, that I should not have been so arrogant to think that it was up to me to make a significant contribution to the future. Great, if that was how it worked out; but my main task was to ensure the continuity, not just of my family but of the things that I believed in. Forget the literal meaning of "begatting," treat it metaphorically. It can apply to institutions and ideas as much as to kith and kin. We are links in a chain, it is up to us to keep things going because who knows which generation will be the one to make the big difference. David came nine generations after Ram.

The definition of a wise person in the Book of Proverbs re-inforces the importance of continuity—he should ensure "that there should be an inheritance for his children's children." Jonathan Rauch, in his insightful book about Japan, *The Outnation,* describes his meeting with Yasunari Hirata, who started a business in 1946 making pushcarts and baby carriages, and is now making industrial robots. Talking of his job, Hirata says, "I see the company as an infinitely growing child. I will die, but it continues to live, and my responsibility is to see to that. And I want to continue to build better and better robots." Rauch goes on to say that the word "profit" would not have passed Hirata's lips if he, Rauch, had not brought it up. "Yasunari Hirata was plainly not particularly interested in profits—not, I mean, in the sense of *taking profits.* He did not live lavishly and he seemed more concerned with immortality than with money." He was expressing something Richard Hooker said in England at the end of the sixteenth century: "The Act of a Publick Society, of men done five hundred years sithence, standeth as theirs, who are presently of the same Society, because Corporations are immortal." These ideas are of long standing.

John Rawls, the philosopher of justice, says, "Each generation must not only preserve the gains of civilization and culture, and maintain intact those just institutions that may have been established, but it must also put in place a suitable sum of real capital appreciation." Long before him, Edmund Burke, writing about the French revolution, said: "Society is indeed a contract. . . . not only between those who are living but between those who are living, those who are dead and those who are to be born."

This is cathedral philosophy, the thinking behind the people who designed and built the great cathedrals, knowing that they would never live long enough to see them finished. The new cathedrals will not be of stone and glass, but of brains and wits. They will take equally long to build and we who start the building may not live to see the conclusion. That is why we need to look beyond the grave and beyond our generation. It is hard to believe that we will make the sacrifices involved unless we can believe in the long-term existence of our little local world and of the bigger global one. We should, however, remember that there is no need for that continued

existence to take the same form as it is in at present. The
second curve is different from the first; there has to be
change to be continuity. Yasunari Hirata started with
push chairs and moved on to industrial robots. We need
to have faith in the future to make sense of the present.

HOW BIG AND FAR
SHOULD WE THINK?

Some would say that even life itself is now under threat,
that Malthus's fears of two centuries ago—that the world
would not have the resources to feed its peoples—are
coming true. The numbers do indeed look frightening,
and the arguments of people like Paul Kennedy, in his recent book *Preparing for the Twenty-First Century,* or Edward
Wilson with *The Diversity of Life,* are horribly convincing,
but the end is not the end if we don't wish it to be. We
may need to adopt the sort of measure that Lester
Thurow suggests, paying rents to the third world for
their forests. This payment might encourage us to develop the millions of different life forms which Wilson iden-
tifies in his book. One way or another, we shall need to
have enough faith and interest in the continuity of the
world and its peoples to give up some of our present
wealth for the unseen benefits of people whom we will
never know.

Some people already have that understanding.
Charles Hampden-Turner argues that Americans see
time sequentially, as a straight line, whereas Orientals see

it as a loop. To many Westerners time, he says, is a running reaper, waving his sickle, but in the East, time comes around again and again. If you take the running reaper view, there is no time to lose, things must be completed before time runs out. In the loop view of things time never runs out; therefore, you want to create self-renewing systems, systems that will still be in place when time, your friend, comes around again, even if you are not there.

We could look at Europe in this light. One way or another Europe has to become more integrated. Its separate countries are too small to go it alone in a world of 8 billion. But for Europe to succeed it must be more than just a convenient arrangement for the exchange of goods. It must be a federal unity with twin citizenship, a separation of powers, and proper subsidiarity. Federalism also requires a common law and, ultimately, a common currency. At the moment, the unequal economies of Europe adjust their currencies when they have to, in order to restore their competitiveness and to allow them to sell their goods. Once there is a common currency, devaluation is no longer possible. Europe will then have to do what individual countries do to equalize their regions—make grants, loans, and tax concessions to help the weaker catch up with the stronger. For Europe to have the cash to do that adequately, we shall probably have to increase the tax which we pay to the center, possibly by a factor of seven or eight. Voters will not be prepared to do that unless their sense of history, of continuity backward and forward, allows them to see themselves as an integral and continuing part of this place called Europe, a place that has been a part of their heritage and a place that will contain the future of their great-great-grandchildren. There will be no short-term rewards for this sort of sacrifice, no way of justifying it within the lifetime of a parliament.

In a business, quarterly reports and an average life span of 40 years for big companies tend to put immortality on the back burner in most boardrooms. Boards always want numbers, but trust no numbers beyond four or five years. It is always safer to put one's money on deposit than to risk building a cathedral of new enterprise. Only family businesses have the urge to think beyond the grave, and even then, probably not beyond three generations. The pressures to do it in your own lifetime seem to be mounting, even though the institutions that currently own our public companies are themselves supposed to have a continuing existence, independent of the people who run them. We need to re-emphasize the fact that institutions can be immortal even if we are not. The Mitsui Corporation and my old Oxford college are both over six hundred years old, both still going strong. You only look ahead as far as you can look back.

Invited to help one large bank create a statement of its vision and values, I looked, to start with, for an understanding of its purpose. "Why do you exist?" I asked. "To make our shareholders seriously rich," the executives replied. Their shareholders were mainly other banks, insurance companies, and pension funds. Had any of these, I asked, ever made that request, or defined what their expectations might be? It appeared not. The chairman added that, after announcing the bank's first ever annual loss some years back, he had thought it right to call on its principal shareholder, an insurance company, to explain the situation. "They were noticeably uninterested," he said. "They seemed to assume that we would be around forever and that this was only a temporary hitch which we would put right." Maybe they were right, I suggested, maybe they wanted to keep their money in a place where it could stay forever. "I think that they are very unusual," he replied, disposing of that suggestion. Immortality as a concept can be frightening. Continuity can, however, be a useful and less scary compromise.

On a more domestic scale, we have to worry about the grandchildren. Now that one in every 2.3 marriages in Britain is ending in divorce, it is not clear who will be thinking about the grandchildren when there will be an abundance of unaccepted step-grandchildren or, looking at it another way, many children with grandparents whom they have never known. Will we, anymore, want to plant trees which take 50 years to mature if we do not know who will be around to look upon them when they are fully grown? More formally, the concept of justice between the generations will be harder to maintain when the generation after next is semi-detached. Families, we used to think, would last forever. It made sense to say "when I am gone," knowing that much would still continue even if it changed. If families become a temporary convenience, or inconvenience, time will indeed run out.

My hopes are fragile ones. We should not, for a start, underrate the power of the millennium idea. It will encourage people to look backward and forward further than they have ever done before. The heritage movement is also gathering pace. We don't pull buildings down so often but refurbish them instead, turning our docks, warehouses, and factories into new uses. That is usefully symbolic. RISC, the International Research Institute for Social Change, reports, from its recent surveys, that, "We can witness an increasing sense of responsibility towards the flux of history, including a greater recognition of the importance of both past and future generations." That is encouraging. The environmental campaigns, particularly the idea of Gaia, of earth as a self-renewing system, take us huge leaps back into history and forward into the future.

If companies, as I hope, rediscover the virtues of membership for their chosen ones, if job hopping becomes more perilous, and if shareholders wield less power, then the corporate world may see a desire for permanence creep in again. Corporate leaders do have influence, so when 48 executives from the largest corporations in the world form the Business Council for Sustainable Development, governments and others will listen. Carl Hahn, as chairman of Volkswagen and a member of that group, wrote in its report: "If we think of the future—a central part of the obligation to rising generations—we must adopt the cyclical approach on which the whole of nature is based." In the marketplace, fashion, that god of the merchandisers, may be losing some adherents, or rather, the new fashion may be to make do with what you have, or to choose what suits you and not your neighbors' fancy. Home-made, second-hand, of good not flashy quality, the stuff that lasts may become the style.

Now that people live longer and four-generation families, with great-grandchildren, become more common, the idea of continuity in a family may yet re-emerge, when today's footloose parents become tomorrow's grandparents and realize what they are missing—a stake in the future. Because we look forward only as far as we can look back, this realization can only come late in life. The rights of grandparents would then become an issue, with children effectively adopted by their grandparents irrespective of their parents' new arrangements.

These are all fragile hopes. One of the most important tasks of leadership is to point to some kind of continuity, both forward and backward. Without that sense of continuity there is no point in sacrificing any of the present for the future.

⓭ A Sense of Connection

We were not meant to stand alone. We need to belong—
to something or someone. Only where there is a mutual
commitment will you find people prepared to deny themselves for the good of others. We, however, in our belief
in liberalism and individualism, are wary of commitments. We look suspiciously at words like "loyalty" and
"duty" and "obligation." Independence, whether we seek
it or not, is being thrust upon us. "Modern society knows
no neighbours," said Disraeli more than a century ago,
and it has been no different since. Loneliness may be the
real disease of the next century, as we live alone, work
alone, and play alone, insulated by our modem, our
Walkman, or our television. The Italians may be wise to
use the same word for both alone and lonely, for the first
ultimately implies the second. It is no longer clear where
we connect or to what we belong. If, however, we belong
to nothing, the point of striving is hard to see.

More crucially perhaps, if we belong to nothing,
there is no reason to make sacrifices for other people.
Duty and conscience have no meaning if there is no

sense of commitment to others, and of others to us. "Think of a person," said Rawls, "without any sense of justice. He would be without any ties of affection, friendship or mutual trust, incapable of resentment or indignation. He would barge into a line if he could get away with it and expect everyone else to do the same. He would be less than human." In a world where so many of the connections which underlay a sense of justice are breaking down, the interesting question is not why some of us are criminals, but why more of us are not.

The workplace has been the central community in the lives of many in this century. Lewis Mumford, extolling the virtues of the monastic community, said: "True leisure is not freedom *from* work but freedom *in* work, and, along with that, the time to converse, to ruminate, to contemplate the meaning of life." Modern work does not provide many of those opportunities, even for those in the core. Even so, the lament of the prematurely retired is usually the loss of community, while the loneliness of the long-distance teleworker is well documented.

If the idea of membership becomes more prevalent for those in the core of institutions, then the workplace will remain a central point of connection for many. That "many," however, is likely to be less than half of the workforce and less than a third of all adults. It is a connection, however, which could be a very isolating one, consuming all one's time and energies, and insulating its members from the surrounding society, unless more attention is paid to the corporate contract with the other stakeholders and more trouble taken to chunk time sensiblly.

One unintended consequence of the organization society was to remove from many of us the need to belong to anywhere other than our workplace. As a result, when we leave it we have nothing. We also substituted the homogeneous communities, which our work provided, for the mixed communities of the old neighborhoods. We replaced the community of place with the community of common interest. When you do that, there is no longer any need to think of sacrificing anything for your new neighbor because your neighbor is in the same position. If we compound that by turning our communities of place, where we choose to live, into equally homogeneous zones, we shall never need to see, meet, or pay heed to anyone different from ourselves.

In 1989, there were 130,000 community associations in the United States, according to the Community Associations Institute, helping to administer the lives of 30 million Americans, one of every eight. Some of these are just small condominium associations, but 80% of them own land as well and have an average of 543 dwelling units. More are on their way and are getting more homogeneous; one new development in Newport Beach has even put a limit on the size of residents' dogs.

There is also the Leisure Hills development in Laguna Beach, California: 21,000 people with their own taxes, security force, television station, and 12 bus routes. Guards at its gates check the identity of all visitors. It, and other ghettoes like it, are the equivalent of the walled cities of medieval Italy. They provide their inmates with the security and peace of mind which they cannot find in the mixed community. They should remember, however, said *The Economist* when reporting this, that those walled cities of Italy were the source and cause of endless wars.

The new ghetto communities are too small and too like-minded to be the basis of a new balance in society. They are only connected to themselves. On the other hand, the nation is too big and amorphous a concept to count as a connection. We are not going to be easily persuaded to make sacrifices for people whom we never see, to pay to clean streets we never walk, or to mend sewers we shall never use. The rich of Surrey may feel sympathy for the poor of Tyneside in the North, but they will not send too much of their money their way, because they will never see the results. The organization society has gradually become the ghetto society, ghettoes of the rich and ghettoes of the poor. We should remember that it was the enclosure acts of Henry VIII in England, passed in order to get better productivity from the better farmers, which forced the poor into poverty and into a new underclass. We need a community large enough to be a mixture and small enough to be visible to all its inhabitants. We need to return to the city-state or at least to the township.

There used, in Britain, to be a thing called civic pride. Town hall would compete with town hall in magnificence and in achievement. Central government down the decades has progressively stripped the cities and the towns of their powers, distrustful of how they used those powers and, in some cases undoubtedly, abused them. All that is now left in Britain of this tradition is the city football club.

There was a time when the municipal universities were the pride of the city fathers, businesses competed to see their names inscribed above a new hall or lecture theater, their sons and daughters studied there, married there, lived and worked there. In the 1950s, the British government decided, in a spirit of liberalism, that it would give fees and maintenance grants allowing students to study at any university in the land. The city universities instantly became national universities. They lost their local identity and their local patronage; students roamed freely, made their contacts and their roots far from the city of their birth. It was done in the name of freedom or, say some, because Oxford and Cambridge wanted to have the pick of all the land. Whichever, it was one more blow against the city-state.

The city may, however, be on the rise again. Europe is fast becoming a Europe of cities. Manchester competes with Barcelona, which competes with Munich, in business and in sport. Airlines fly from city to city, not only from capital to capital. Cities twin with cities. It makes good sense. We can identify and connect with a city, even if we only live in its hinterland. The castle, the cathedral spire, or even its office blocks are a visible reminder of its presence. The city is a community on a human scale, the nation-state is not. The only people who wave the Union Jack these days, or the French Tricolor for that matter, are drunken sports fans. As the middle orders disappear in a more integrated Europe, the city is replacing the nation-state as the focus of our identity and our way of connecting with society.

But our cities are a mess. They represent the extremes of riches and poverty, of affluence hobnobbing with squalor. They look to be an unlikely basis for community. It is for that reason that they should be given back the responsibility for their futures. In Britain the bulk of the income of the cities comes from the central government. The cities are only the delivery agents. Proper subsidiarity means that they have the right to decide on their own priorities and have both the authority and the means to deliver these.

Cities, together with their hinterlands, are the best basis for the Chinese contracts. Only in that size community will it be possible to harness the talents and the money of the more successful in order to provide investment in the infrastructure and help for the less fortunate. Those who give will be able to see the results of their donations or their taxes. In a city you can make a difference in your spare time. At the national level making a difference is a career. Giving the cities more responsibility also means giving them the right to raise the money to deliver that responsibility. There lies the rub, because central government in all countries, save perhaps Canada, likes to take the first and largest bite of the tax pie. It will require a radical central government to give up this extent of fiscal control.

America's cities are further down the road than most European ones, but everywhere there are encouraging signs. The idea of an annual European City of Culture has begun to catch the imagination. Cities, rather than countries, are promoting themselves as centers for tourism and development. They compete for heritage and environmental awards. Cairo, with 15 million people, recently received a United Nations award for recycling its rubbish, proving that size need be no drawback to civic pride. Only London, among the world's large cities, has no government of its own, no center for civic pride.

The hard truth is that federations should be both small and big, with the inevitable result that the middle levels fade. One day Europe will be a federation of cities in all but name. When it is, it will mean more to each of us to be a European because every city will need to rely on Europe and its connections far more than they do today. Reciprocity, too, is easier when there are many different players. It is easier for Glasgow to exchange people or projects with Oporto than with Birmingham because it is less directly competitive. It is also more fun for both. The idea of twin citizenship is, it seems, easier to foster on a city basis than a national one.

I have long cherished the idea that at age 13 every child in Europe should spend a semester at a school and in a home in another European country. If done universally, the only cost would be the travel. This is something that would be hard to negotiate or organize on a national basis. It could be done more fruitfully with a city-to-city scheme. Nothing would do more to heighten a young person's sense of history and of a shared destiny than such a connection.

For Europe read North America, because surely, one day, geography and economic logic will create a new and larger federation there, bringing in Mexico and Canada. That, too, will need to be broken down into cities and large towns rather than nations or even states, if the rich are ever going to be prepared to shell out for the poor. Twinning and swapping will help create a sense of shared history and destiny. Japan and Southeast Asia may, one day, feel the same pull to be both larger and smaller, if they are to compete with the growing force of China.

Most of the hope for cities, however, rests with the organization, particularly the organizations of business. Businesses need the cities, they need the educational and cultural resources the city offers in order to attract the quality of people whom they will need in their core. They will need the transport connections cities alone can offer. They need the plethora of small service businesses and portfolio people who congregate on the edges of cities, in the new-style villages. They need the buzz of cities, their energy and excitement, the variety of life, the contacts, and the political connections. Paradoxically, the trend at present is the other way. Organizations are flee-ing to the country or the suburbs, seduced by the dream of the office or factory in a garden, bringing the work to the workers, relying on telecommunications to give them their link with the outside world. They are creating their own walled cities in the woods.

They may re-think this approach. The new federal dispersed organization does not have to have many people in any one place. Local work centers and tele-clubs can proliferate in the woods and the suburbs but the city needs part of their action and they need the city for its connections. Only when the organizations return will they be prepared to invest in making these hubs of humanity civilized once again because they have the clout, the spending power, and the leadership skills to do so. Compromise may be the way forward. The symbolic analysts increasingly will work in more places than one, live in more places than one, not *rus in urbe*, the classicist's dream of the country in the town, but *rus et urbs*, for they will need them both. It is when the rich as well as the poor live in the cities and the towns again that there will be a chance that the rich will help pay for the education and the transport of the poor. It will ultimately be in their interest to see their city better educated and there-fore richer.

If organizations do not re-think and re-locate, we shall see the cities declining even faster, those of power and influence retreating still further into their walled vil-lages and insulating themselves from anyone unlike them-selves. That way there is no balance, less chance of sacri-fice or compromise, less likelihood of turning paradox into progress. It is, therefore, heartening to know that the businesses of London are creating a program for Lon-don, that those of Birmingham are doing likewise, as are the leading citizens of Atlanta, Seattle, Barcelona, Se-ville, Glasgow, and many more. Federations, said Os-borne, are the laboratories of democracy. Some of our cities may yet, unexpectedly, find ways to re-connect us with our neighbors. Where they lead others may follow, if, that is, those who rule in the center come to appreci-ate the benefits of federalism.

VIRTUAL
CITIES

Great cities are made up of small villages. The truth is
that we need both our village and our city. We need both
the comfort of friends and the stimulus of strangers. We
relax in the company of people like us, but need a connection with difference, both to keep us awake and to
make us feel part of something bigger. Only then will
conscience prevail over self-interest, and duty over comfort. Villages, even villages of like-minded and like-
income people, in the midst of great cities, would be a
good basis for a fairer society. For most of us it will not
happen like that. Our cities will not change fast enough.
We must create our own virtual villages and cities, communities that one can describe but that do not necessarily belong to any one place.

The family has always been one of our "villages."
The traditional family is no longer so traditional, but
there are still families. They may not be composed of conventional relationships, and there may be more step-
relations than blood relations, but there are still families.
The extended family is now horizontal as well as vertical,
covering a wider group of people of the same generation
and offering a wider choice of soul mates than the nuclear
family of old. These new "virtual families," which include close friends and partners as well as blood relations, may well be more comfortable villages than the
older model. We should not despair of the family, but redefine it.

Work was another of those villages, often, as I have
suggested, a ghetto unconnected with the world outside,

but a comfortable way of connecting with like-minded colleagues. The spread of the minimalist organization is making these connections more difficult, as more people move or are moved outside. Increasingly, modern-day portfolio workers have to create their own "virtual organization" made up of clients and occasional partners or co-workers.

The virtual organization can be glimpsed in the new "clubs" for the independent portfolio workers. One of these clubs is provided by the intermediary employers, the employment agencies, who are the brokers for the portfolio workers, just as agents are for actors, writers, and models. The intermediary employers, or agents, provide a reference point, a base and an ally, even if it is only at the end of a telephone line. There are also the networks of contacts that any independent soon builds up, the job clubs for the unemployed, and the professional associations for those qualified to belong to them. My son, an independent actor, has both an agent and his "filofax club" of contacts. These are his virtual organization between engagements. One new development is the teleclub, a building designed to be used by the occasional teleworker, offering cubicle space, receptionist services, food and drink, and all the necessary communications equipment.

Some organizations provide their people with a local regional office. Other facilities are for rent by individuals by the day, week, or month. There are more up-market versions in the city offering meeting and eating rooms for rent by strangers, or more formal clubs that restrict their facilities to members. Hotels, airports, and railway stations have seen the commercial potential in the new form of work, and provide their own teleclubs for travelers with a gap in their schedule. In time, these places may offer a form of temporary fellowship as well as a facility, becoming a physical embodiment of the virtual work village.

There are other virtual villages. One study, delightfully called "Organizing Around Enthusiasms," discovered there were 315 organizations in one Surrey suburb devoted to hobbies, interests, sports, and other enthusiasms, all run by volunteers, all doughnuts with a core of organizers and a space full of subscribers and participants. They offer scope for activity, these places, not paid work, but they also provide an opportunity to take comfort in the company of friends, a temporary village.

These virtual villages need to be complemented by virtual cities, opportunities to meet and be challenged by strangers. Mickey Kraus advocates more use of what he calls "third places," places like cinemas, churches, shopping malls, and other common meeting arenas. More could be done to make these third places into opportunities for connecting with strangers. Too often they are only lonely crowds. We cannot rely on them but need to do more to build our own connections with strangers. This is difficult and challenging but not impossible. It is best done by collecting a portfolio of atypical villages.

My brother-in-law retired from his full-time job in business. He looked for part-time work for four days a week. Four years later, he thinks he might manage to fit in an occasional day. He is far too busy to do more. He is a local magistrate, a governor of a local school, and a member of the parish council; he sits on various committees of the local judiciary and the police authority, runs the local gymkhana and part of the big agricultural show in his part of the world. Instead of one rather monotonic business organization he now belongs to a wide range of groups. He sees sides of life that were probably undreamed of in his business office. Like him, we can use the new flexibility of work and life to make more connections than we would have in the days when one organization kept us fully occupied for most of life.

A portfolio of community activities, be they good works or good enthusiasms, is the antidote to ghetto life, be the ghetto a country village, a fenced city in California, or a slum in an inner city. You do not have to have my brother-in-law's background to serve the local community. Some of the best school governors, the best tribunal members, and the best youth leaders come from deprived areas. They have an understanding and a grip on reality that outsiders can only envy. Our community organizations promote the connections across the divides, both horizontal and vertical.

"There is no such thing as society," said Margaret Thatcher. She meant that individuals could not hide behind "society," looking to it to provide for them or to protect them. "Individualism," said John Maynard Keynes, "if it can be purged of its defects and abuses, is the best safeguard of individual liberty." But the "if" in Keynes's statement is important. The sense of connection in a mixed community is the best means of purging those defects. There can be a beneficial compromise between the individual and a community. Society does exist and is necessary, but as a supplement to individualism, not a substitute. Society is also an outlet for our contributions, a place to give to as well as to receive.

We get more local as we get older and often feel the need to give something back to society, in time and expertise rather than money. As long as they don't hide away in their geriatric shrubberies and golf gardens with their size-restricted dogs, the early retirees have a lot to give, but they will want to do it locally, where they can see some of the results. We could leave a new corps of para-professionals, individuals basically trained and competent enough to help with the youth service in schools, in hospitals and clinics as counsellors or drivers or attendants, as dispensers of benefits and welfare, as researchers for projects or coordinators of volunteers. Some of this is happening already, more could happen if civic pride were resurrected everywhere. We cannot wait for central government to give away its power; we have to do what we can without it. In the world ahead we shall increasingly have to make our own connections, our own virtual city.

A Sense of Direction

In the end a sense of continuity and of mixed connections will not be enough to give point to striving. Maybe nothing will. Francis Fukuyama, the author of *The End of History and the Last Man,* put it this way:

> The end of history will be a very sad time. The struggle for recognition, the willingness to risk one's life for a purely abstract goal, the worldwide ideological struggle that called forth daring, courage, imagination, and idealism, will be replaced by economic calculation, the endless solving of technological problems, environmental concerns, and the satisfaction of sophisticated consumer demands. In the post-historical period there will be neither art nor philosophy, just the perpetual caretaking of the museum of human history.

Fukuyama's argument is that liberal democracy, the tolerance it brings with it, and the affluence that made it possible, have removed the will to fight great causes. We slump in comfort. When we compete it is for the World Cup or for gold medals. Such things do not bring forth great art or noble deeds, they don't stir the heart more than momentarily, nor do they foster revolutions. Like dogs, if we are well fed, we are content. When scientific and economic progress lead more societies into the contentment stage we shall see the end of history.

Democratic societies are tolerant; they do not tell their citizens how they should live, or what will make them happy, virtuous, or great. It is not an accident that people in democratic societies are preoccupied with material gain and with the myriad small needs of the body. Nietzsche, who deplored this state of being, said that "the last man" has "left the regions where it was hard to live, for one needs warmth." "One still works," he goes on, "because work is a form of entertainment. But one is careful lest the entertainment be too harrowing. One no longer becomes rich or poor: both require too much exertion. Who still wants to rule? who obey? Both require too much exertion. No shepherd and one herd! Everybody wants the same, everybody is the same: whoever feels different goes voluntarily into a madhouse."

There are no great causes anymore. We fill in our resumés in the hope that they may be the pathways to a style of life to which we feel accustomed. It is hard to detect great, unfulfilled longings or irrational passions just beneath the surface of the average first-year law associate. We have to find a source of pride in sports or eccentricities instead. We are all last men now.

On the other hand, we may not like the end of history when we see it. Fukuyama again: "Self-interest rightly understood came to be a broadly understandable principle that laid a low but solid ground for public virtue in the United States. . . . But in the long run those values had a corrosive effect on the values . . . necessary to sustain strong communities and thereby on a liberal society's ability to be self-sustaining." Hegel understood that the need to feel pride in one's humanness would not be satisfied by the peace and prosperity that comes with the end of history. In 1806, he wrote, "We stand at the gates of an important epoch, a time of ferment . . . when a new phase of the spirit is preparing itself." Almost two hundred years later we are in another time of ferment, another dark wood. It may not yet be the end of history.

Maslow was right when he postulated that there was a hierarchy of needs, that when you had enough material goods you moved your sights to social prestige and then to self-realization. If it stopped there, however, life would remain too self-centered, too egotistical. The hierarchy needs another step. Maslow recognized this himself, toward the end of his life. In the preface to *Toward a Psychology of Being*, he accepted that he had been mistaken, that self-actualization is not the ultimate end, and that we need something "bigger than we are, to be awed by and to commit ourselves to."

FOR THE SAKE
OF A CAUSE

If we are not machines, random accidents in the evolutionary chain, we need to have a sense of direction. Tolstoy, in his confessions, tells how he could find no logical purpose for his existence. He was successful, happily married, rich, yet it all seemed pointless. He concluded that man only lived because he believed in something. If he didn't believe there was anything there, he would kill himself. Faith, therefore, was "the power of life." Laura Ashley, explaining why she started her country fabrics business, said: "I sensed that most people wanted to raise families, have gardens and live as nicely as they can." Her business flourished in the 1970s and into the 1980s because I think she caught the mood of the times, the generation of the last men. Mayor Dinkins of New York City, however, at Arthur Ashe's memorial service in 1993 said: "Service to others is the rent we pay for our space on earth. Arthur Ashe paid his rent in full."

Mayor Dinkins, in his turn, may have caught the mood of the approaching millennium. The RISC survey, cited above, identified a growing search for meaning and authenticity as the distinguishing element of the mood of the 1990s, in contrast with the "boring generation" of the 1970s and 1980s—"people uninterested in ideological debate and more concerned about themselves." This new ethical dimension had, they said, several manifestations—"a sense of purpose, a search for identity, dignity and a quality of life prior to lifestyle (aesthetics and harmony)."

It is a search for a cause. The cause, however, to be truly satisfying must be a "purpose beyond oneself," because to be turned in on yourself, said St. Augustine, is the greatest of sins; because we discover ourselves through others, said Jung; because the immortality, for which we all privately long, is really immortality through others. This last statement needs some justification because it suggests that most of the religions have got it wrong. There may be an existence after death, for all we know, but it will certainly not be expressed in bodily shape, or in time or in space. It is, therefore, literally inconceivable, and, as a result, not something which I myself can take seriously. My purpose in this life, as I read the teachings of the sages, is to so live that others can live better after I have gone, that, if I live on in any sense, I may live on in the continuing lives of others. Heaven and Hell I see as medieval forms of social control, along with theories of reincarnation.

Kierkegaard tells my favorite religious story: an Indian man of deep religion was making his way home to his village in the hills when there was an avalanche and the fallen mountain barred his way. Devout man that he was he got down and prayed to his God to move the mountain, and waited there in faith. Ten years later, still there, still praying, still blocked by the mountain, he died, still believing. In the village they still talk of him as the "man who waited for the mountain to move." Kierkegaard's point is that God does not move mountains, in spite of what the Bible says, but that we have to climb the mountains, with His help. But first, we have to identify the mountain; we must find the cause which lifts us beyond ourselves.

The mountain does not have to be an Everest. We do not need to change the world. To nudge a little bit of it along will be enough. One owner-manager of a bakery once contacted me. "I want to make my little company the best in the country," he said. "What do you mean by best?" I asked. "Are you talking profits?" "Only up to a point," he replied. "Without some longer-term profitability I won't be able to keep it going, but that's not really the point—I want it to be a showcase, the kind of company which I and all who work there will be proud to say, 'That's my place.'" He had a cause. Art Fury, of Post-it fame, commenting on entrepreneurial success said once, "Those who invest only to get rich will fail; those who invest to help others will probably succeed."

Those who talk about vision as essential for the future of an enterprise are right, but it has to be the sort of vision that others can relate to. Not many in the lower realms of the organization can get excited by the thought of enriching the shareholders. "Excellence" and "quality" are the right sort of words, but they have been tarnished by repetition in too many organizations. They were often synonyms for cost or people cutting, or they begged the question—for whom are we doing this? We need to believe in what we are doing if we are to lift ourselves onto a second curve in any enterprise, or if we are going to be prepared to compromise our wishes and our needs for the good of others. Some businesses turn this into a concern for the customer, but we have to wonder whether their concern is not a means rather than an end, a more effective way of doing business.

I once attended a top-management seminar arranged by a leading group of hotels. The keynote speech was given by a Benedictine monk who explained St. Benedict's view of hospitality. In his monastery, he said, they had many visitors, both men and women, who came for peace and reflection. We try to practice St. Benedict's command to welcome every man, each man, and the whole man. That means, he explained, that we do not discriminate between president and pauper (every man), and we had both last month; we treat each person as an individual (each man), paying attention to their special needs and wishes; last, we try to deal with the whole of them, with their deep needs as well as their surface wants, and to enter as fully as they will let us into their lives. His talk was rapturously received by the executives who saw in it a reason for their hard work, a reason more deeply satisfying than numbers on a balance sheet. When, however, I checked in later to their hotel, I found that every moveable item was attached in some way to the walls. Even the toilet roll in the lavatory was in a locked container. "We have to," they explained to me. "Our visitors will steal anything given half a chance." If you can't trust your visitor with the toilet roll, I reflected, it will be hard to deliver the Benedictine message. Yet for a moment they had glimpsed a vision, a direction worth the journey.

As George Bernard Shaw put it, in *Man and Superman:*

> This is the true joy in life, the being used for a purpose recognized by yourself as a mighty one; the being a force of nature instead of a feverish, selfish little clod of ailments and grievances complaining that the world will not devote itself to making you happy.

Britain will never be "great" again, in the sense of being a world power or an economic force, but she could find a new cause and forge a new existence as, for instance, the "Athens of Europe," meaning the old Athens of learning, culture, and the arts. Her great comparative advantage is her language. Everyone, everywhere, wants to learn it. Her universities, theaters, designers, artists, architects, movie and TV filmmakers, writers and the *literati,* musicians, and dancers are world class. Sadly, she is more likely to be known as a museum than as a cultural center, but the opportunity is there to find a second curve and to lift her people, to give her a sense of new direction.

Malaysia now boasts a 2020 Vision. The pun is deliberate. It is a 30-year plan, outlining the kind of place the country's leaders would like to see it be in 2020. It is underpinned by an optimistic rate of growth—7.2%, enough to bring it up to American standards of living by 2020—but that is where it starts, not where it stops. The vision is full of the ways in which that money will be spent and distributed, on education, on the handicapped, on the old, on the environment (belatedly). Visiting that country I expected cynicism, instead I found excitement. Business leaders had a justification for their efforts. Others had hope. The headlines of the plan were even pinned up in taxis.

It is hard, in a comfortable democracy, to find a cause which lifts the efforts of the comfortable ones. That is why some fear a return to war as a way of putting some energy back into our peoples. Making money not war has turned out to be less inspiring. Another war would be a wasteful way to disprove the end-of-history thesis. It is tempting to call for better leadership, but we probably expect too much from the leaders of the nations. Those nations are too big, the connections not strong enough, the commitment to the future not long enough. It is better to look smaller, to our now smaller organizations, to local communities and cities, to families and clusters of friends, to small networks of portfolio people with time to give to something bigger than themselves. We have to fashion our own directions in our own places.

A Postscript

My wife's ancestor was Sir Rowland Hill, famed as the in-
ventor of the penny post and the first postage stamps in
the 1840s. Until he came on the scene, letters were
priced according to their weight and the distance they
had traveled, rather logically when you think about it,
and were paid for by the recipient. A letter from London
to Edinburgh, for instance, might cost 1 shilling and six-
pence, a lot of money in those days, but then it was a
long distance. Some clever folks used to send an empty
envelope to their families, who would then refuse to pay
for it on arrival because they had heard what they
needed to hear, that their loved one was alive. That put
the costs up even more. The result was that only the rich
could afford to send real letters to each other. Letter writing was an elite pastime.

Rowland Hill proposed that we do some upside-
down thinking. If every letter cost only one penny, no
matter where it went to in Britain, and if it was prepaid

by a "stamp" which you could buy in advance and stick on, he argued that two things would happen: first, the volume of mail would expand enormously, more than compensating for any loss on the cost of the longer deliveries, but, more important, everyone would be able to send letters. This would give an enormous boost to education because there would be a practical point in everyone learning to read and write. It would also help the cohesion of the nation because friend would be able to keep in touch with friend, mother with son, wife with distant husband. It would be, he said, not just a commercial success but a significant piece of social reform.

Nobody believed him. It took years of argument and campaigning before he convinced Parliament to make the change. When they did, the results were dramatic. Within ten years some 50 countries had adopted the idea of pre-bought stamps and the modern postal service was born. Rowland Hill died richly honored and is remembered to this day as the father of the penny post.

What is really interesting about this story, however, is this: when he started his campaigning, Rowland Hill was not in the postal service. He was a clerk in the South Australia Commission, having, before that, been a schoolteacher in his father's school. The postal service was none of his business. He was not rich, nor famous, nor influential, but he cared; he saw something that needed to be done and he decided that he could not live with himself if he didn't do something about it. We can't wait for the mountain to move, we have to climb it ourselves.

We are not all destined to be social reformers. Richard Harries, the Bishop of Oxford, tells another story. There was a rabbi once, called Zuzya of Hannipol. He spent his life lamenting his lack of talent and his failure to be another Moses. One day God comforted him. "In the coming world," He said, "we will not ask you why you were not Moses, but why you were not Zuzya." We are not gods. We can't do everything, or even very much at all, in the small interval of time we have in this world. It is as much as we can do to be our full selves, full doughnuts.

FIRES IN
THE DARKNESS

There are two photographs on my desk, taken by my wife in South Africa. The first is the head of a small black boy. He is smiling; everything about his eyes and his face radiates intelligence, enthusiasm, excitement. It is a happy face, full of promise. The second photograph is of the same boy, but this time the photographer has moved back, so that you now see him full length. You see the shanty behind him, his bare feet, and the excrement in which he is standing. The two photographs may be a symbol of our challenge today, not only in South Africa. The intelligence and the promise is there if we can only release it from the chains of its surroundings.

Our people are clever, many of them. Most people are decent, given half a chance. They are not uncaring, if only because they know that a world which crumbles around them will do them no good at all. But first there has to be a general acceptance that the world has changed. The end of communism does not mean that capitalism, in its old form, is therefore the one right way. The triumph of the democracies over totalitarianism does not mean that everything in those democracies is thereby validated. The huge strides made by science in the past decades does not mean that scientists have, or could have, the answer to everything and that the rest of us need not bother.

It is also the end of the age of the mass organization, the age when we could all confidently expect to be employed for most of our lives if we so wanted, and over 90% did so want. Work will still be central to our lives but we shall now have to rethink what we mean by work and how it might be organized. At first sight, the challenge is daunting, but work in those mass organizations has never been unalloyed bliss for all. The mass organization has not been with us that long. We should not think of it as a law of nature. Maybe we shall be better off without it.

The hope lies in the unknown, in that second curve if we can find it. The world is up for re-invention in so many ways. Creativity is born in chaos. What we do, what we belong to, why we do it, when we do it, where we do it—these may all be different and they could be better. Our societies are built on case law. Change comes from small initiatives which work, initiatives which, imitated, become the fashion. We cannot wait for great visions from great people, for they are in short supply at the end of history. It is up to us to light our own small fires in the darkness.

Acknowledgments

There is an invisible corps of people behind this book.
They are the individuals who are out there living the
lives and driving the organizations that I try to describe.
Some of their problems and achievements, their hopes
and their frustrations, I hear from their own lips in semi-
nars, conferences, and private sessions. Some I glean
from the writings of others, in journals, newspapers, and
books. These people must remain anonymous, unless
they have chosen to write publicly about their world, but
I owe them a debt of gratitude because it is through their
stories that I glimpse reality.

I have learned a lot from the writings of others, be
they management theorists, old philosophers, or modern
thinkers. Most of those whom I have cited in the text
have their relevant works listed in the bibliography. That
bibliography also contains some authors not specifically
mentioned in the text but whose writings have been particularly influential as I worried about the theme of the
book. It is a small recognition of my gratitude to them.

I have had the pleasure of working with two publishers simultaneously, in London and Boston. No one can serve two masters, it was said, but I have found it enormously helpful to be exposed to two sets of views and comments, particularly when they come from such insightful people as Gail Rebuck and Paul Sidey in London and Carol Franco and Natalie Greenberg in Boston. They, and every member of their teams, have been perfect midwives to this book during its rather prolonged birth pangs. I am forever grateful for their interest in the book, their patience, and their encouragement.

My family know all too well the problems of living with a writer. They have been wonderfully tolerant of my moods, have allowed me to parade parts of their lives in the book, and have been tactful critics of the work in progress. My wife's consistent belief in me and in what I am trying to do has been a particular source of strength, seeing me through the valleys of self-doubt, because writing is a lonely business most of the time. To Liz, Kate, and Scott go my love and thanks.

Diss, Norfolk, England.
September 1993

Bibliography

bbeglen, James C., and George Stalk, Jr. *Kaisha, the Japanese Corporation.* New York: Basic Books, 1985.

lbert, Michel. *Capitalism Against Capitalism.* London: Whurr, 1993.

nderson, Digby, ed. *The Loss of Virtue.* London: Social Affairs Unit, 1993.

ppleyard, Brian. *Understanding the Present.* London: Pan Books, 1992.

aden-Fuller, Charles, and John Stopford. *Rejuvenating the Mature Corporation.* London: Routledge, 1992.

ahrami, Homa. "The Emerging Flexible Organization." *California Management Review,* Summer 1992.

all, Christopher. "The Adelphi Idler." *RSA Journal,* May 1993.

ennis, Warren. *An Invented Life.* Reading, Mass.: Addison-Wesley, 1993.

ishop, Jeff, and Paul Hoggett. *Organizing Around Enthusiasms.* London: Comedia, 1988.

loom, Allan. *The Closing of the American Mind.* New York: Simon & Schuster, 1987.

ommission for Social Justice. *The Justice Gap.* London: IPPR, 1993.

rucker, Peter. *Post-Capitalist Society.* Oxford: Butterworth-Heinemann, 1993.

ukuyama, Francis. *The End of History and the Last Man.* London: Hamish Hamilton, 1992.

albraith, John K. *The Culture of Contentment.* London: Sinclair Stevenson, 1992.

ardner, Howard. *Frames of Mind.* New York: Basic Books, 1985.

ortz, P. *A Critique of Economic Reason.* London: Verso, 1989.

oyder, George. *The Just Enterprise.* London: Andre Deutsch, 1987.

ammer, Michael, and James Champy. *Re-engineering the Corporation.* New York: HarperCollins, 1993.

Hampden-Turner, Charles. *Corporate Culture*. London: Hutchinson, 1990.

Havel, Vaclav. *Disturbing the Peace*. New York: Vintage Books, 1991.

Hegel, G. *The Philosophy of History*. London: Dover, 1956.

Henzler, H. A. "Eurocapitalism." *Harvard Business Review*, July–August 1992.

Hewitt, Patricia. *About Time*. London: Rivers Oram Press, 1993.

Jay, Antony. *Corporation Man*. Hammondsworth: Penguin, 1975.

Kanter, Rosabeth Moss. *When Giants Learn to Dance*. London: Simon & Schuster, 1989.

Keegan, William. *The Spectre of Capitalism*. London: Radius, 1993.

Kennedy, Paul. *Preparing for the Twenty-First Century*. New York: Random House, 1993.

Kester, W. Carl. *Japanese Takeovers*. Boston: Harvard Business School Press, 1991.

Kraus, Michael. *The End of Equality*. New York: Basic Books, 1992.

Leinberger, Paul, and Bruce Tucker. *The New Individualists*. New York: HarperCollins, 1991.

Lucas, J. R. *On Justice*. Oxford: Clarendon Press, 1980.

Nietzche, F. *Beyond Good and Evil*. New York: Vintage Books, 1968.

O'Neil, John R. *The Paradox of Success*. New York: Putnam, 1993.

Osborne, David, and Ted Gaebler. *Re-inventing Government*. Reading, Mass.: Addison-Wesley, 1992.

Pascale, Richard, and Anthony G. Athos. *The Art of Japanese Management*. New York: Warner Books, 1982.

Peters, Tom. *Liberation Management*. New York: Alfred A. Knopf, 1992.

Rauch, Jonathan. *The Outnation*. Boston: Harvard Business School Press, 1992.

Reich, Robert. *The Work of Nations*. New York: Alfred A. Knopf, 1991.

Sampson, Anthony. *The Essential Anatomy of Britain*. London: Hodder and Stoughton, 1993.

Savage, Charles. *Fifth Generation Management*. Bedford, Mass.: Digital Press, 1990.

Schor, Juliet B. *The Overworked American*. New York: Basic Books, 1992.

Schumacher, Fred. *Small Is Beautiful*. London: Harper & Row, 1983.

Schwartz, Peter. *The Art of the Long View*. New York: Doubleday, 1991.

Semler, Ricardo. *Maverick*. London: Hutchinson, 1993.

Senge, Peter. *The Fifth Discipline*. New York: Doubleday, 1990.

Shames, Laurence. *The Hunger for More*. New York: Times Books, 1989.

Stayer, Ralph. "How I Learned to Let My Workers Lead." *Harvard Business Review*, November–December 1990.

Stewart, Rosemary. *Choices for the Manager*. London: McGraw-Hill, 1983.

Thurow, Lester. *Head to Head*. New York: William Morrow, 1992.

Trompenaars, Alfons. "The Organization of Meaning and the Meaning of Organization." Doctoral diss., The Wharton School, University of Pennsylvania, 1987.

Waldrop, M. Mitchell. *Complexity*. New York: Simon & Schuster, 1992.

Watkinson Report. "The Responsibilities of the British Public Company." London: British Institute of Management, 1972.

Wilson, Edward O. *The Diversity of Life.* Cambridge, Mass.: Harvard University Press, 1993.

Young, Michael. *The Rise of the Meritocracy.* London: Penguin, 1961.

Index

national income
  accounting for, 227–229
  nature of, 222–226
National Insurance of Britain, 80
Nation at Risk, A, 199–200
networks, 219. *See also* agents
New Zealand, 228
Nietzsche, Friedrich, 274
nonprofit organizations, 154,
  183–184
noun skills, 207, 209

Occam's Razor, 141
OECD, 26
Office of Information of Britain,
  128
Ogilvie Benson Mather, 231
Okun, Arthur, 89
O'Neil, John, 58
organizations. *See also* business
  attitudes toward work in, 21–24
  balance sheets of, 229–234
  biggest, 181
  cities as resources for, 266–267
  compromise in, 90–94, 95–97
  current status of, 15
  curvilinear logic in, 60–63
  devising second sigmoid curve
    in, 57–59
  effects of doughnut principle on,
    70–71, 79–84, 85
  effects of work hours on, 28–29,
    31
  leaders of second sigmoid curve
    in, 64–67
  management of paradox in,
    11–12
  meaning of business in,
    151–154
  nature of sigmoid curve in,
    50–51
  paradoxical nature of, 34–36,
    41–42, 286
  personal fulfillment in, 77
  subsidiarity in, 134–139, 141,
    142–248

twin citizenship in, 116, 120–
  127, 129–130
virtual, 35–36, 39, 138,
  269–272
"Organizing Around Enthusi-
  asms," 270
Osborne, David, 128, 267
Ostroff and Smith, 136
O'Toole, James, 168
Outnation, The (Rauch), 250–251
Overworked American, The (Schor),
  29–30
Owen, David, 90–91
Ownership of business, 154, 161
  institutional, 174–177
  limited liability in, 173–174
  membership, 189–192
Oxford University, 254

paradox
  of aging, 36–37
  definition and management of,
    11–14
  framing confusions of, 17–18,
    41–43
  of individual, 38–39
  of intelligence, 18–21
  of justice, 39–41
  of organizations, 34–36
  of productivity, 24–27
  of riches, 32–34
  of time, 27–32
  of work, 21–24
Paradox of Success, The (O'Neil), 58
parental leave, 29
part-time employment
  in America and Europe, 22–24
  for new parents and before re-
    tirement, 29
Pascale, Richard, 121
Pearce Report, 232
pension funds, 176
pension plans, 162, 163, 164
Percy, Eustace, 190
personal doughnuts, 75–79, 85
personal income. *See also* income